W0105944

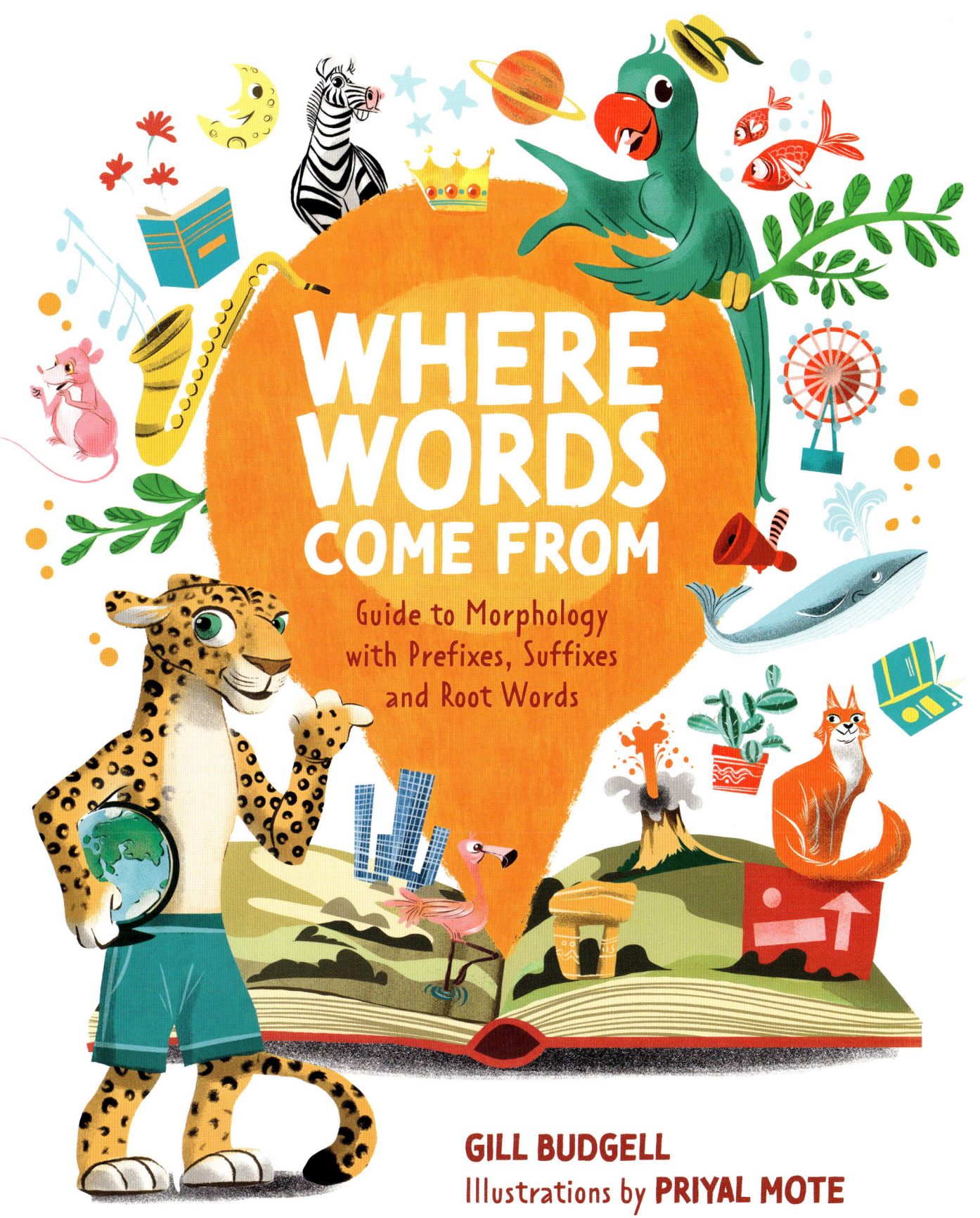

DK SUPER

WHERE WORDS COME FROM

Guide to Morphology with Prefixes, Suffixes and Root Words

GILL BUDGELL

Illustrations by PRIYAL MOTE

Penguin
Random
House

Author Gill Budgell
Illustrator Priyal Mote

Produced for DK by
Emma Forge, Tom Forge
Designforge.ink

Publisher Sarah Forbes
Managing Editor Katherine Neep
Managing Art Editor Sarah Corcoran
Senior Editor Amelia Jones
Production Editor Sachin Gupta
Production Controller Isabell Schart

First published in Great Britain in 2025 by
Dorling Kindersley Limited
20 Vauxhall Bridge Road
London SW1V 2SA

The authorised representative in the EEA is
Dorling Kindersley Verlag GmbH. Arnulfstr. 124,
80636 Munich, Germany

Copyright © 2025 Dorling Kindersley Limited
A Penguin Random House Company
10 9 8 7 6 5 4 3 2 1
001–344510–Feb/2025

All rights reserved.
No part of this publication may be reproduced, stored in or
introduced into a retrieval system, or transmitted, in any
form, or by any means (electronic, mechanical, photocopying,
recording, or otherwise), without the prior written permission
of the copyright owner.

A CIP catalogue record for this book
is available from the British Library.

ISBN: 978-0-2417-1171-2

Printed and bound in China

www.dk.com

MIX
Paper | Supporting
responsible forestry
FSC™ C018179

This book was made with Forest
Stewardship Council™ certified
paper – one small step in DK's
commitment to a sustainable future.
Learn more at www.dk.com/uk/
information/sustainability

Contents

Introduction

What is **morphology?**

Morphology is the study of how words are formed and their relationship to one another.

---

morph means "shape or form"

ology means "the study of"

So morphology is the study of the shape or form of words.

What are **morphemes?**

But what are words made from? They are made up of morphemes, which are the smallest unit of meaning within a language.

Morphemes can be:

- **words that carry meaning**, for example, nouns, adjectives and adverbs
- **words that relate to grammar**, for example, prepositions ("in", "on", "under"), conjunctions ("and", "but", "so"), and articles ("a", "an", "the")
- **word-forming parts of language that help us create new words** or change the function of a word. These are prefixes that are added to the front of a word or root, and suffixes that are added to the end of a word or root (appear: disappear, appearance)
- **word-forming parts of language that change the amount, tense, or degree** of something (for example, plural 's' to change a word from singular, meaning just one, to plural, meaning more than one)

5

The importance of learning about **morphology**

Improve your **vocabulary**

If you know that words are made up from smaller units of meaning, it may help you decode new words and learn new words, too. If you know that "quest" means "to seek or search", it may help you understand, read, or write related words like "question", "questionnaire", or "unquestionable".

In the same way, you can use your knowledge about the building blocks of words to make connections between words that may seem unrelated. If you read a series of books about a character's "quest", you may remember the meaning of "quest", and it will tell you that these stories are about a character's search for something.

So morphology can help you to extend your vocabulary, to talk about things more accurately, and to make good word choices, too.

Improve your **spelling**

Breaking words down into smaller chunks is probably already something you try to do when you aren't sure how to spell a word. Knowing a bit more about the standard building blocks of words will help you make more accurate chunks.

So, imagine you want to spell a word like "miscommunication".

If you don't know about morphology, you may split it like this: mis–com–uni–cay–shun... oops!

But if you know about morphology, you will think like this:
mis (prefix), *communicate* (verb), *ion* (suffix)

And you will know that when you add the suffix *ion*, the word usually drops the *e* before adding *ion*.

You are more likely to split the word like this:
mis + *communicat(e)* + *ion* = *miscommunication!*

Sometimes morphemes can be spelled differently when they appear in words – look out for examples within this book.

DID YOU KNOW?

Ad infinitum is a Latin-based phrase meaning to "to infinity or "forever". When the character Buzz Lightyear in the film *Toy Story*, said, "To infinity and beyond!", he could have said "Ad infinitum!" instead. Either way, it means the possibilities are limitless.

Improve your **reading** and **comprehension**

When you are reading and you come across a tricky word, morphology can help you decode it more accurately. Just like chunking is used in the example on the previous page for spelling "miscommunication", it can be applied to chunking words while reading.

You can split a word by syllables, look for prefixes and suffixes, and spot word families. You become a kind of word detective, solving the challenges of reading as they arise.

If you aren't struggling to decode words, it means that you can grasp the meaning of what you are reading more quickly and efficiently. The flow of your reading, known as **reading fluency**, will improve and so too will your understanding of what you are reading, which is known as **comprehension**.

And if you are reading fluently and with comprehension, you are more likely to enjoy what you are reading. This is called **reading for pleasure**. It's when you find the joy of curling up with a book and getting stuck into a really good story, or digging deep into a book that gives you facts and information about something that fascinates you.

Make **learning languages** both fun... and easier!

Being a word detective is fun. Morphology helps you detect language patterns, make connections, and make better predictions and word choices. It's a bit like building your own internet of words and meanings. If you don't believe me, have a look at the morpheme maps starting on page 158.

Knowing more about words and where they come from will give you confidence in speaking, reading, and writing. When one word leads you to another and another, *ad infinitum*, you will become hooked!

Finally, if you know about or speak another language, you will already have realised that languages can be linked to each other. If you aren't that person, then don't worry, you will see this very soon. Throughout this book, words are flagged with icons to tell you whether they originate from Greek, Latin, or Old English. If you know about Greek-based languages or Latin-based languages, the meanings of many words will be clearer for you.

Similarly, if you are going to learn languages at school, knowing more about the origins of words and how they link to other languages will give you an advantage. And who doesn't want to look clever at school?

How **English** developed

Etymology is the study of where words come from (their origins) and how their meanings have changed throughout history.

Experts think there is no single reason for language development.

People move from place to place for work, to share ideas, to find a better place to live, and to experience new cultures. They bring their food, their books, their religions and their traditions. The language for all these things travels with the people.

In this way, English has been influenced by many other languages throughout its history.

The oldest foundational roots of English, from thousands of years ago, are from a group of languages called *Indo-European*. It may seem unlikely, but it means that some words from languages like Hindi, Spanish, and Russian have shared connections with English. There is also a connection with a group of languages like German and Dutch, called *West Germanic* languages.

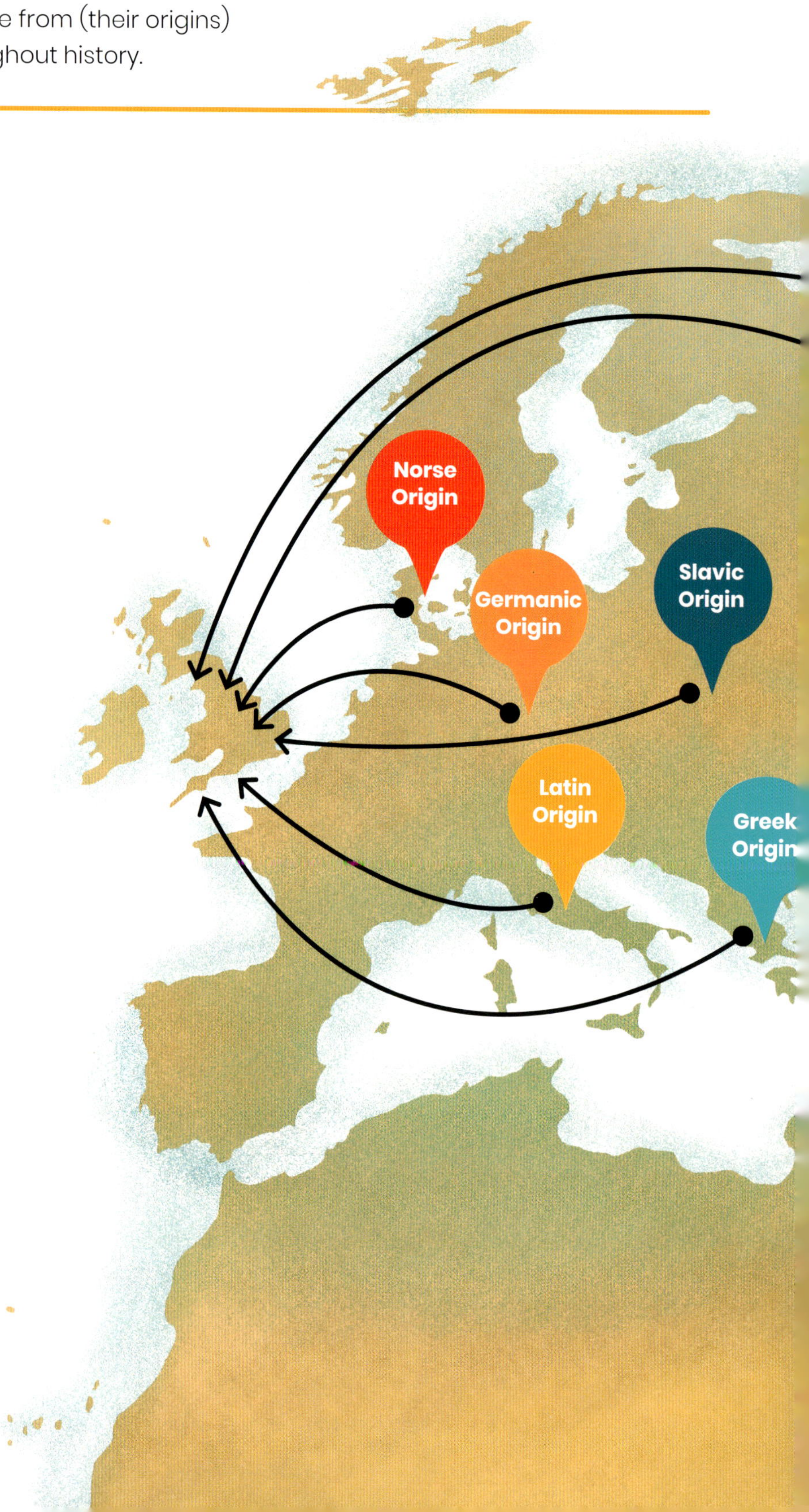

Norse Origin

Germanic Origin

Slavic Origin

Latin Origin

Greek Origin

DID YOU KNOW?

The English word "night" looks like this in other languages:
noch in Russian
nacht in German
noche in Spanish

The similarity is quite clear to see. These kinds of links are called cognates. Cognates are words that have the same origin, or are related and similar in some way.

Iranian Origin

Indic Origin

Old English
origin

DID YOU KNOW?

Experts say that Icelandic (the language spoken in Iceland) is close to the Old English used by Anglo-Saxons and the Old Norse used by Vikings.

In this book you will sometimes see the **Old English** icon to indicate that a word has Germanic roots. Old English was the form of English used by Anglo-Saxons around the 5th century. This formed the core of English as we know it today.

Slightly later, Vikings travelled the globe to find new lands and raid the treasures of people living there. They brought new influences and words with them. When they invaded Britain, the local people spoke **Old English** and the Vikings spoke **Old Norse**. Over time, words from Old Norse mixed with Old English, creating a new variation of English.

Many words we use today come from Old Norse. For example: *kaka* meant "cake", *hreindyri* meant "reindeer", and *kalla* meant "to call".

Middle English
origin

DID YOU KNOW?

The word "conquest" is linked to Old French and to Medieval Latin. It means "to win with effort".

Later again, during the 11th century, William the Conqueror from Normandy in France arrived in England with his army. They fought a long and harsh battle near Hastings. They won the battle and, over time, massively transformed the English language that the Anglo-Saxons had created. Norman French became the language used by the powerful. The less powerful continued to speak English, and Latin was used for religious purposes. This was the time when many French words were introduced into the English language, and it is sometimes called **Middle English**.

FUN FACT!

The Battle of Hastings was fought between the army of William, Duke of Normandy and the army of King Harold Godwinson in 1066, and it is known as one of the longest battles in medieval history. This conquest is known as the Norman Conquest and William as "William the Conqueror" because William and his army won the battle.

Latin and Greek origin

FUN FACT!
The stories of Greek mythology provide English with many expressions. If you have the "Midas touch", it means you are lucky, because Midas was a king in Greek mythology who could turn everything he touched into gold.

DID YOU KNOW?

During the Roman Empire (43–410 CE), Britain was conquered and ruled by the Romans. Despite almost four centuries of Roman rule, Latin had little impact on the English language at that time.

Like Latin, Greek was originally the language of philosophy, mathematics, and science. But unlike Latin, Greek is still a language spoken in many forms across the world. Historians think that more than 150,000 words of English are derived from Greek.

Many words in English have their origins in Latin and Greek. You will see these icons throughout the book.

Thousands of years ago, Latin was the language of religion, science, and scholars.

Although the language is no longer spoken today, its influence is still very strong in modern languages all over the world, including English.

How English is still developing

Like most languages, English is always changing and still borrowing from other languages. Around 60 per cent of English words have origins from other countries and their languages.

Every year, publishers of English dictionaries announce a "Word of the Year". People can vote for the word, and it is supposed to be a word that is likely to survive over time. Some of the most recent words have included "selfie" and "vax". Each year, new words are added to dictionaries so they keep current.

Definitions

Base words

Root words

Prefixes

Suffixes

Nouns

Verbs

Adjectives

Adverbs

Syllables, syllable stress and phonemes

Base words

A **base** word is a stand-alone English word that has meaning. It can form other words by adding suffixes and prefixes or can remain a word when they are removed.

---

agree is a **base** word. It has its own meaning and is a stand-alone word, but we can also add prefixes and suffixes to make words that are linked to it and its meaning:

dis + **agree** = **disagree**

dis + **agree** + ment = **disagreement**

agree + able = **agreeable**

In this book you can discover base words in the prefixes and suffixes sections starting on page 74. That's where we show you how to make new words using prefixes and suffixes.

Root words

The **root** of a word carries its meaning and tells us if the word originates from **Latin**, **Greek**, or **Old English**. It plants the word in soil so that it can grow when suffixes and prefixes are added. Although it may not always stand alone as a word in its own right, it's ready to grow.

---

dict is a Latin **root** word. It has its own meaning, "speak", but is not a stand-alone word. It needs prefixes or suffixes to create words with meaning. You can read about *dict* on page 47.

pre + **dict** = **predict**

dict + ate = **dictate**

dict + ion + ary = **dictionary**

Prefixes

A **prefix** is added to the beginning of a base word or a root word to make a new word with a linked or similar meaning. It is made up of a letter or a group of letters.

We reuse **prefixes** over and over again with different words because they too carry meaning. Some prefixes, like *dis*, have a negative meaning and so change a word from a positive, "agreement", to a negative, "disagreement".

In this book you can read about some of the most common prefixes relating to **negativity**, **time**, **direction** or **position**, and **size** or **amount**, starting on page 74.

Suffixes

A **suffix** is added to the end of a base word or a root word to make a new word with a linked or similar meaning. It is made up of a letter or a group of letters.

We reuse **suffixes** over and over again with different words because they too carry meaning. Some suffixes are added to nouns and are called **noun suffixes**. They are appendages. Some are **verb suffixes**, and there is a section in this book starting on page 134 that dedicates its pages to exploring some of these. **Adjective suffixes** are unmissable starting on page 138, and **adverb suffixes** are quietly tucked away on page 147.

Nouns

A **noun** is a word that refers to a person (**Sam**), place (**London**), thing (**light**), event (**party**), substance (**soil**), or quality (**happiness**).

Proper nouns are the names of people, places, or objects and are spelled with a capital letter. For example, "Sam is in London."

Countable nouns are words that represent things that can be counted, for example, "I study 13 subjects at school." We use the word "fewer" with these types of nouns because we can count them: "I wish I could study fewer subjects at school!"

Uncountable nouns are words that represent things that cannot be counted, for example, water. We use the word "less" with these types of nouns because we cannot count them: "That plant needs less water!"

We can create nouns from other types of words by adding a **noun suffix**. Look at these words:

teach + **er** = **teacher**

pian(o) + **ist** = **pianist**

enjoy + **ment** = **enjoyment**

You can further explore how to use suffixes to make nouns starting from page 117.

Verbs

A **verb** is a word (**listen**) or a phrase (**stand up**) that describes an action, how you feel (sometimes called a state), or what you're experiencing (sometimes called an event). Most verbs in English are main verbs, but some verbs are called **auxiliary verbs**, and in English these are: **be**, **do**, and **have**. They are used before a main verb. For example, "We are learning." ("are" is from the auxiliary verb "be", and "learning" is from the main verb "learn").

Verbs have a basic form that changes when you want to change who it relates to by changing the pronoun (I jump, she jumps), or what time it relates to by changing the tense ("I am skipp**ing**, they skipp**ed** yesterday, and we'**ll** all **skip** tomorrow").

Many verbs follow patterns or rules and are **regular** (chew ➡ chewed). Some verbs are **irregular** (eat ➡ ate).

Adjectives

An **adjective** is a word that describes a noun. We can describe an apple as delicious ("It's a **delicious** apple").

We can add a prefix to an adjective to change it into a different meaning:
in + edible = **inedible**
("It's an **in**edible apple")

We can add a suffix to an adjective to change it into a noun:
sweet + **ness** = **sweetness**
("The apple is sweet; its sweet**ness** is delicious")

We can add a suffix to an adjective to make it into a verb:
ripe(n) + **ing** = **ripening**
("The ripe apple"; "The apple is ripen**ing**")

Adverbs

An **adverb** is a word that adds more information about a verb. But it can also add more information to an adjective or another adverb, and sometimes a clause or a whole sentence.

"Be careful! Cross the road **safely**."

"The crossing is **extremely dangerous**." (adverb, adjective)

"Cross the road **really carefully**." (adverb, adverb)

We can add a suffix to a word to make an adverb. In this book you can further explore these adverb suffixes including *ly*, *wards*, *ways*, and *wise*.

"Never walk **backwards** when you are crossing the road."

Syllables, syllable stress, and phonemes

A **syllable** is either a whole word or one of the parts that a word can be split into. It usually contains a vowel. You can easily clap syllables.

CHALLENGE!

Clap the word "clap". It has one syllable. Clap the word "windmill". It has two syllables. Clap the word "bungalow". It has three syllables.

Remember that counting the syllables within a word is not the same as counting the phonemes (the smallest units of sounds in word) to work out what graphemes (letters) to write.

The vowels in syllables can be stressed or unstressed. Stressed syllables are said with strength and emphasis. Unstressed syllables are weak and said without emphasis. Many words contain the schwa sound. It is an unstressed vowel syllable and is usually voiced as "uh". You can hear it at the end of the word "general", in the middle of the word "family", and in the first syllable of the word "tomorrow". It's like a shrug of the shoulders!

DID YOU KNOW?

If you are trying to spell a word, you might need to move from clapping syllables towards making a choice of phonemes that represent graphemes. This is called segmenting a word or encoding.

Word	Number of claps/syllables	Syllable stress	Number of phonemes	Sound buttons to show phonemes
clap	1	clap	4	c l a p
power	2	**pow**-er	3	p ower
energy	3	**en**-er-gy	5	e n er g y
disappointment	4	dis-a-**ppoint**-ment	12	d i s a ppoint ment

Spelling rules

Adding s to make plural nouns

Other irregular plurals

Talking (and reading and writing) about the "here and now"

Talking (and reading and writing) about the past – regular and irregular

Confusables

Adding s to make plural nouns

Have a look here at the basic rules for changing a singular noun into a **plural noun**. That means we change from talking about one thing to talking about two or more things. And when we do that, we often have to change the spelling.

CHALLENGE!

What is the plural of these words?

berry, cup, sandwich, box, boy

berries, cups, sandwiches, boxes, boys

Rules	Singular noun	Plural noun	Example sentence
Most words just add **s**	balloon	balloon**s**	There were balloons of all shapes and sizes.
But look out for this exception!	child	child**ren**	The children were excited.
Add **s** if the word ends in a vowel + **y**	toy	toy**s**	The children were given lots of toys.
Add **ies** to words ending in a consonant + **y**	puppy	pupp**ies**	The puppies were very soft to cuddle.
Add **es** to words ending in **s** or **ss**	hiss	hiss**es**	The children could hear the snake's hisses.
Add **es** to words ending in **ch**	watch	watch**es**	The children wore their new watches.
Add **es** to words ending in **sh**	sash	sash**es**	The children wore party sashes.
But look out for this exception!	fish	fish	The fish all swam happily.
Add **es** to words ending in **x**	fox	fox**es**	There were pretend foxes at the petting zoo.

Adding s to make **plural nouns** for words ending in a, i, o, and u

If a word ends in a vowel, there are a few rules that you can use to guide you.
Remember that the vowels in English are a, e, i, o, and u.

Rules	Singular noun	Plural noun	Example sentence
Most words ending in vowels, **a**, **i**, **o**, and **u** just add **s**	camera	camera**s**	They took pictures with their phone cameras.
	kiwi	kiwi**s**	The kiwis were delicious.
	banjo	banjo**s**	There were banjos.
	kangaroo	kangaroo**s**	The kangaroos played the banjos.
	emu	emu**s**	The emus played the drums.
But look out for this exception!	potato	potato**es**	The flamingos ate potatoes.
And look out for this exception!	spaghetti	spaghetti	There was plenty of spaghetti for everyone.

DID YOU KNOW?

If you are struggling to remember the vowels in English, try this! **A**crobatic **E**lephant **I**n **O**range **U**nderwear. If you don't like that phrase, try making up your own.

Adding s to make **plural nouns** for words ending in f and ff

For words ending in f and ff, you can use these rules below as a guide for adding s.

Rules	Singular noun	Plural noun	Example sentence
Most nouns ending in **f** drop the **f** and add **ves**	loaf	loa**ves**	There were different loaves.
Nouns ending **ff**, just add **s**	cliff	cliff**s**	They could see the cliffs far away.

Other **irregular plurals**

Rules don't always work! This table shows some of the words that are irregular because the plural is formed in different ways.

Rules	Singular noun	Plural noun	Example sentence
Some change the middle vowel(s)	m**a**n	m**e**n	The men chatted.
	m**ou**se	m**i**ce	The mice hid by the log.
	g**oo**se	g**ee**se	The geese flew overhead.
Some add letters	child	child**ren**	The children ran in the field.
Some change letters	fung**us**	fung**i**	They did not see the fungi.
	antenn**a**	antenn**ae**	They could see the butterfly's antennae.
Some do not change	deer	deer	The deer were on the hillside.

Talking (and reading or writing) about the "**here and now**"

When we are referring to the "**here and now**", we use the present tense. Look at the tables below to see some of the rules for regular and irregular verbs.

Use the present tense for talking about	Example sentences beginning with I (first person)
Routines and habits	I play football every week.
Doing things now or in the very near future	I'm playing football now.
	I'm playing football tomorrow.
Describing what you think or feel	I feel excited about the football match.

Using the present tense with he, she, or it (third person)	Verb +	Example sentences
Most often we just add **s** Say /**z**/	play + **s** plays	She play**s** football. Say: She play**z** football.
Add **ies** if the verb ends in **y** after a consonant Say /**eez**/	carr**y** – y carr + ies carries	She carr**ies** a bag for her kit. Say: She carr**eez** a bag.
Add **es** if the verb ends in: **s**, **ss**, **sh**, **ch**, **x**, or **o** Say /**iz**/	coa**ch** + **es** coaches	She coach**es** football. Say: She coach**iz** football.
	stre**ss** + es stresses	Before the match, she stress**es**. Say: She stress**iz**.
	rela**x** + es relaxes	After the match, she relax**es**. Say: She relax**iz**.

Talking (and reading or writing) about **the past**

Look at the table below to see some of the rules for regular and irregular verbs in the **past simple tense**.

Regular verbs: most often we just add ed		
If a verb ends in **p**, **s**, **sh**, or **k**, add **ed** Say /**t**/	jum**p** + ed jumped	We jump**ed** over the bench. Say: We jump**t**.
If a verb ends in **t** or **d**, add **ed** Say /**id**/	lif**t** + ed lifted	He lift**ed** a weight over his head. Say: He lift**id**.
If a verb ends in **b**, **n**, **v**, **m**, **z**, or **oy**, add **ed** Say /**d**/ (if regular!)	ai**m** + ed aimed	I aim**ed** at the target. Say: He aim**d**.
If a verb ends in **e**, just add **d** Say /**d**/	wav**e** + d waved	She wav**ed** at her parents in the crowd.
But look out for irregulars!	see saw	They **saw** their friends.
If a verb ends in **y**, replace the **y** with **ied**	worr**y** – y worr + ied worried	We worr**ied** when it started to rain.
If a verb ends in a vowel and a consonant, double the consonant	st**op** + ped stopped	The team coach stop**ped** us from getting too excited.

See a list of irregular verbs on page 171.

24

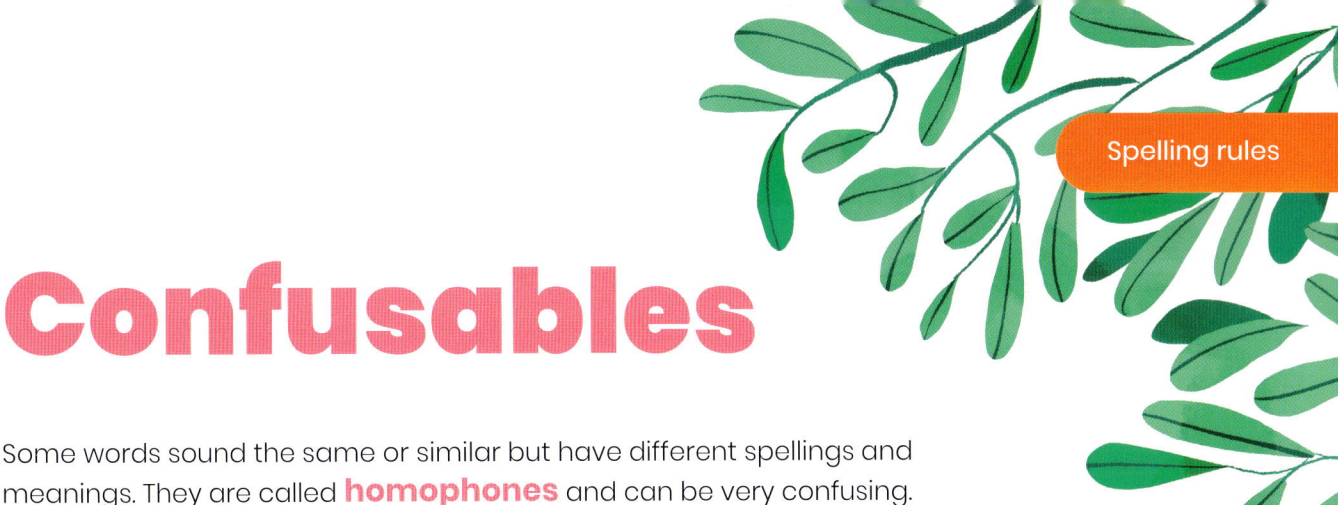

Confusables

Some words sound the same or similar but have different spellings and meanings. They are called **homophones** and can be very confusing.

Using an apostrophe to merge two words is called a **contraction**. Contractions can also be very confusing.

Words	Example sentences
accept/except	I **accept** your apology, **except** I still feel upset.
affect/effect	What you say **affects** me. The **effect** is positive.
bought/brought	I **bought** you this. Good thing I **brought** it with me!
business/busyness	My parents have a family **business**. We are busy – there's always so much **busyness** in my family.
compliment/complement	Thank you for the **compliment**. I'm glad you think that lime green **complements** my hair colour.
mist/missed	There is a **mist** over the hills. I've **missed** that view.
pair/pear/pare	I've picked a **pair** of **pears** and I'm going to **pare** them with my knife.
principle/principal	The **principle** of not running in the hallway is clear when the **principal** says it like that.
stationery/stationary	I'm getting out my **stationery** set to do some writing while this train is **stationary**.
there/their/they're	**There** are quite a few spelling rules. They are writing them in **their** books. I hope **they're** not confused.
to/too/two	I spoke **to** my friend. She is going to the festival, **too**. That means the **two** of us can go together.
which/witch	**Which** book is your favourite? *The Worst* **Witch** or **Which Witch** *is* **Which**?
who's/whose	**Who's** looking for me? **Whose** sunglasses are these?
wonder/wander	I **wonder** if you know how it feels to just **wander**.
your/you're	**Your** favourite song as a toddler was, "If **you're** happy and you know it."

Latin roots

Words related to the body and people

LATIN
ORIGIN

caput

Meaning: **to do with the head**

caput is a root word in words with a meaning related to the head. This doesn't always mean your literal head!

capital city

cap + ital + city
Literal meaning: head city

the main city of a country where the government sits

capital letter

cap + ital + letter
Literal meaning: head letter

the form of an alphabetical letter used to begin a sentence or proper name

chapter

c(h)ap + ter
Literal meaning: little head

one of the parts that a book is divided into

carni

Meaning: **to do with flesh**

carnival

carni + val
Literal meaning: flesh farewell!

a festival

carnation

carn + ation
Literal meaning: flesh colour

a plant with white, pink, or red flowers

carnivore

carni + vore
Literal meaning: flesh eating

any animal (including humans) that eats the flesh of other animals

DID YOU KNOW?

Originally, carnival literally meant "flesh farewell!" or "removing meat" from the diet before a festive time. The word was first evidenced in 1590 as meaning feasting and partying.

cor/cordi

Meaning: **to do with the heart**

cor or **cordi** is a root word linked to words that mean "heartfelt" or "coming from the heart" – the place of kindness.

ac**cord**

ac + cord
Literal meaning: to be of one heart

agreement

dis**cord**

dis + cord
Literal meaning: apart from the heart

disagreement

cordial

cordi + al
Literal meaning: of or for the heart

friendly

DID YOU KNOW?

The noun "cordial" can mean a drink or medicine that stimulates the heart, but these days we usually say "juice".

coll

Meaning: **to do with the neck**

collar

coll + ar
Literal meaning: necklace, band, or chain for the neck

the part of a shirt or coat that fits around the neck and is usually folded over

collared

coll + ared
Literal meaning: capture by the collar or neck

grabbed someone by the collar or neck

collarbone

coll + ar + bone
Literal meaning: neck bone

the clavicle

dent/dens

Meaning: **to do with the teeth**

dent or **dens** is a root word in lots of other words that have a meaning related to teeth.

dentist

dent + ist
Literal meaning: tooth person

a person who is qualified to examine and treat people's teeth

in**dent**

in + dent
Literal meaning: to give something teeth

to give something a jagged or toothed appearance

dandelion

dan (dent/tooth) + de (of) + lion
Literal meaning: tooth of the lion

a wild plant that has yellow flowers with lots of thin petals and jagged leaves

DID YOU KNOW?

"Indent" can also mean to make a written formal contract. An "indented contract" was a written or typed document presented in two identical sections that were joined by a zigzag line. Like a row of teeth!

manu/mani

Meaning: **to do with the hand**

manicure

mani + cure
Literal meaning: hand care

a treatment for hands or nails involving softening the skin and cutting and polishing the nails

manipulation

mani + pul + ation
Literal meaning: a handful of skill

skilful handling control

manual

manu + al
Literal meaning: relating to the hand

a handbook that tells you how something works or how to do something

FUN FACT!

People in ancient Egypt had manicures and used dyes and paints to colour their whole fingertip rather than just the nail. The colour related to their status in the community.

nas

Meaning: **to do with the nose**

nasal

nas + al
Literal meaning: of the nose

relating to the nose and its functions

nozzle

nozz + le
Literal meaning: little nose

a narrow piece fitted to the end of a hose or pipe to control the flow of what is coming out

nostrils

nos + trils
Literal meaning: nose holes

the two openings at the end of the nose

DID YOU KNOW?

nas is a root word that forms all or part of a number of "nose-related" words including "nasturtium", which is the name for a group of plants like watercress. Its name translates to English as "nose-twist" because its smell is so strong it "twists the nose"!

or

Meaning: **to do with the mouth**

oracy

or + acy
Literal meaning: the literacy of the mouth

speaking and understanding speech

orifice

or + ifice
Literal meaning: mouth-making

an opening or a hole, especially of the body

usher

ush + er
Literal meaning: person at the mouth of a building

someone who stands at an entrance of a building or room as a guide

oss

Meaning: **to do with bone**

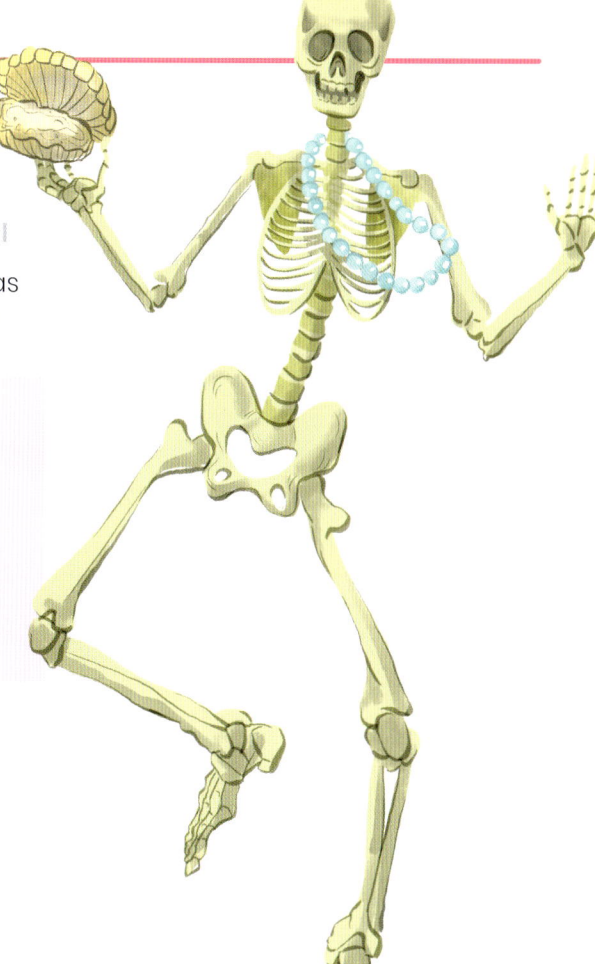

osteology

osteo + logy
Literal meaning: bone science

the study of the structure and function of bones

ostracise

ost(rac) + ise
Literal meaning: to exclude by voting on tiles or pottery

to banish or exclude people from society or favour

oy**s**ter

o(y)s + ter
Literal meaning: bone shell

a large flat, shellfish that has an irregularly shaped shell

FUN FACT!

The ancient Greeks ostracised people for 10 years by public vote if they were thought to be dangerous to society.

ped

Meaning: **to do with the foot/feet**

pedestrian

ped + estrian
Literal meaning: one on foot

someone who is walking

pedicure

pedi + cure
Literal meaning: footcare

a toenail-cutting and skin-softening treatment for the feet

pedal

ped + al
Literal meaning: trick of the foot

a lever in a car, or on a bike or machine, that you press to control the car, bike, or machine

CHALLENGE!

What do you think a pedometer measures?

_____

steps

collect

Meaning: **to gather into one place or group**

collector

collect + or
Literal meaning: one who gathers together

a person or thing that collects

collection

collect + ion
Literal meaning: gather together

a group of things

cull

cull
Literal meaning: choose, select

to pick out or select in order to discard

FUN FACT!

Collectors collect all sorts of things, but to be "officially amazing", according to Guinness World Records, you have to spend years researching and collecting. As of 2024, the largest collection of video games consists of 24,268 items collected over 40 years!

civis

Meaning: **to do with being a citizen**

civis is a root word used with words to do with citizenship or being a good citizen. You may study citizenship at school.

CHALLENGE!

What is the name of the oldest civilisation?
a. Mesopotamia
b. Ancient Peru
c. Ancient India

a

civil engineer

civil + engineer
Literal meaning: one who guides civilians

a person who creates, improves, and protects the environment in which we live

civilisation

civil + isation
Literal meaning: a state of order

a human society that has its own social rules and regulations

city

cit + y
Literal meaning: community of citizens

any large town or urban centre with its own government and administration

humanus

Meaning: to do with being human

humane

human + e
Literal meaning: civil

kind

human rights

human + rights
Literal meaning: the rights of an earthly human

basic human rights that many societies believe all people should have

inhumane

in + human + e
Literal meaning: not civil

cruel

DID YOU KNOW?

Did you know that you have human rights? The United Nations Convention on the Rights of the Child states that every child should be recognised, respected and protected as a unique and valuable human being.

genus

Meaning: to do with race, kind, or birth

generation

gen + er + ation
Literal meaning: race or kind

people born in the same time period

generic

gen + er + ic
Literal meaning: of a general kind

general rather than specific

generous

gen + er + ous
Literal meaning: of noble birth or stock

unselfish

FUN FACT!

Did you know that if you were born after 2010 and before 2024, you are called Generation Alpha – are you a Gen Alpha kid?

populus

Meaning: **to do with people**

popul**ar**

popul + ar
Literal meaning: belonging to the people

enjoyed by a lot of people

popul**ation**

popul + ation
Literal meaning: a people

all the people who live in a country or region

pop

pop
Literal meaning: popular appeal (shortened form of "popular")

music or other form of culture

CHALLENGE!

Which country has the biggest population on Earth?

India

socius

Meaning: **companion or ally**

soci**ety**

soci + ety
Literal meaning: community

a group, club, or community

socio**logy**

socio + logy
Literal meaning: the study of society

the study of the structures and development of human societies

soci**able**

soci + able
Literal meaning: to join closely as companions

enjoying the company of others

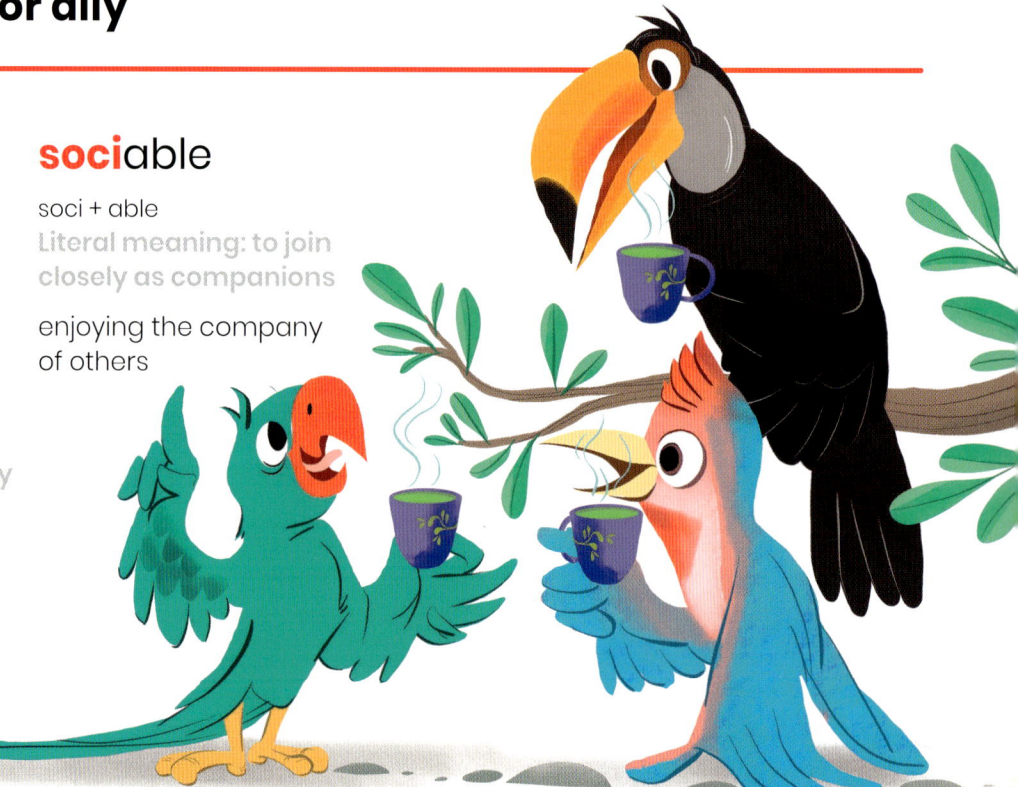

Greek roots

Words related to number

GREEK
ORIGIN

mon

Meaning: **oneness**

monarchy

mon + archy
Literal meaning: the ruling of one

rule by one person with supreme power

monastery

monas + tery
Literal meaning: a place to live alone

a building or home for monks

monolith

mono + lith
Literal meaning: one stone

something made from a single block of stone

FUN FACT!

The longest reigning monarch in the world is thought to be Louis XIV of France, who was crowned at age 4 and reigned for 72 years and 110 days. He died in 1715.

di

Meaning: **two**

dichotomy

di + chotomy
Literal meaning: to cut in two

a division into two parts

diphthong

di + phthong
Literal meaning: having two sounds

two vowel sounds pronounced as one gliding sound

dilemma

di + lemma
Literal meaning: two ideas

a difficult choice between two different options

tri

Meaning: **three**

Try (and that's a different kind of "try") to remember that **tri** is a root word that links to anything to do with three. It's as easy as one, two, three!

triangle

tri + angle
Literal meaning: three angles

a geometric figure having three angles and three sides

tripod

tri + pod
Literal meaning: three legs

a stand with three legs that is used to support something

tricycle

tri + cycle
Literal meaning: three wheels

a pedalled vehicle with two wheels at the back and one at the front

tetra

Meaning: **four**

tetrad

tetra + d
Literal meaning: group of four, the number 4

a group or set of four

tetrapod

tetra + pod
Literal meaning: four legs

any vertebrate with four limbs

tetragon

tetra + gon
Literal meaning: four angles or corners

an uncommon word for a shape with four angles and four sides

CHALLENGE!

What is another word for a shape with four angles and four sides? Clue: think about the word "quad".

"quadrangle" or "quadrilateral"

pent

Meaning: **five**

pentagon

penta + gon
Literal meaning: five angles or corners

a shape with five angles and five sides

pentagram

penta + gram
Literal meaning: five letters or characters

a five-pointed star or shape

pentathlon

penta + thlon
Literal meaning: the contest of five exercises

an athletics competition in which each person must compete in five different events in one day

FUN FACT!

The original Greek pentathlon involved jumping, sprinting, discus, spear throwing and wrestling. A modern version involves swimming, fencing, horse riding, cross-country running and shooting.

hex

Meaning: **six**

hexagon

hexa + gon
Literal meaning: six angles or corners

a shape with six angles and six sides

hexagonal

hexa + gonal
Literal meaning: having six angles or corners

having six angles and six sides

hexapod

hexa + pod
Literal meaning: six legs

anything that has six legs, including insects

FUN FACT!

A hexapod robot is an insect-like, six-legged walking robot. It is stable and can perform different actions.

hept

Meaning: **seven**

heptagon

hepta + gon
Literal meaning: seven
angles or corners

a shape with seven angles
and seven sides

heptathlete

hept + athlete
Literal meaning: contestant
in seven games

an athlete who competes in
a heptathlon

heptathlon

hept + athlon
Literal meaning: the contest
of seven exercises

an athletics competition in
which each person must
compete in seven different
events in one day

FUN FACT!

The events in a
heptathlon are: 100-metre
hurdles, shot put, high
jump, 200-metre run,
long jump, javelin throw,
and 800-metre run.

octo

Meaning: **eight**

octagon

octa + gon
Literal meaning: eight angles
or corners

a shape with eight angles
and eight sides

octopus

octo + pus
Literal meaning: eight foot/
feet

a sea creature with eight long
tentacles

octogenarian

octo + genarian
Literal meaning: eight times ten

a person who is 80 years old

DID YOU KNOW?

October used to be the
8th month of the Roman
calendar. There were
only ten months in the
calendar and the first
month of the year
was March.

ennea

Meaning: **nine**

ennead

ennea + d
Literal meaning: nine

a group of nine things

enneagon

ennea + gon
Literal meaning: nine angles
or corners

a shape with nine angles
and nine sides

enneagram

ennea + gram
Literal meaning: nine letters
or characters

a nine-pointed star or shape

dec

Meaning: **ten**

decade

dec + ade
Literal meaning: ten parts

a period of ten years

decagon

dec + agon
Literal meaning: ten angles
or corners

a shape with ten angles
and ten sides

decathlon

dec + athlon
Literal meaning: the contest
of ten exercises

an athletics competition in
which each person must
compete in ten different
events over two days and
score over 7,000 points

10

CHALLENGE!

Which events are in a
decathlon?

100-metre run, long jump,
shot put, high jump,
400-metre run, 110-metre
hurdles, discus throw, pole
vault, javelin throw, and a
1,500-metre run

hect

Meaning: **a hundred**

hectare

hect + are
Literal meaning: 100 areas of land

a metric measurement of land (10,000 metres squared)

hectogram

hecto + gram
Literal meaning: 100 grams

a metric measurement equal to 100 grams (3.5 ounces)

hectometre

hecto + metre
Literal meaning: 100 metres

a metric measurement equal to 100 metres

FUN FACT!
A hectare is about the size of an international rugby pitch or a baseball field.

kilo

Meaning: **a thousand**

kilograms

kilo + grams
Literal meaning: 1,000 grams

a metric unit of weight equal to 1,000 grams (2.2 pounds)

kilometre

kilo + metre
Literal meaning: 1,000 metres

a metric unit of distance or length equal to 1,000 metres (0.62 miles)

kilobyte

kilo + byte
Literal meaning: 1,000 units

a measurement of storage in a computer system equal to 1,000 bytes

CHALLENGE!
If kilobyte is abbreviated to KB, and kilogram to kg, what is the abbreviation for kilometre?

km

41

mega

Meaning: **a million, great, or large**

megabyte

mega + byte
Literal meaning: a million units

a unit of computer storage space equal to a million bytes

megaphone

mega + phone
Literal meaning: great voice

a funnel shaped device to increase the volume of the voice and direct it

megastructure

mega + structure
Literal meaning: a very big build

a very large and/or tall building or buildings

giga

Meaning: **a billion or giant**

gigabyte

giga + byte
Literal meaning: a thousand million units

a measurement of storage in a computer system equal to 1 billion bytes

gigantic

giga + ntic
Literal meaning: giant

extremely large

gigawatts

giga + watts
Literal meaning: a thousand million watts

a unit of electrical power equal to 1 billion watts

DID YOU KNOW?

Gigabytes are abbreviated to GB and gigawatts to GW.

poly

Meaning: **many, more than one**

polychrome

poly + chrome
Literal meaning: many-coloured

having more than one colour

polyglot

poly + glot
Literal meaning: many tongued

a person fluent in many languages

polygon

poly + gon
Literal meaning: many sides

a shape with three or more straight sides

FUN FACT!

Rainbows contain at least seven visible colours (red, orange, yellow, green, blue, indigo, and violet), so "polychromatic" would be a very good description of them!

arithmo

Meaning: **number, counting, or amount**

arithmetic

arith + metic
Literal meaning: the counting art

the science of numbers

log**arithm**

log + arithm
Literal meaning: ratio number

the number that shows how many times a number has to be multiplied by itself to produce another number

arithmetical

arith + metical
Literal meaning: according to the rules of arithmetic

having to do with numbers

FUN FACT!

Around 1765, arithmetic was part of "mathematical arts". The mathematical arts were considered to be arithmetic, geometry, music and astronomy.

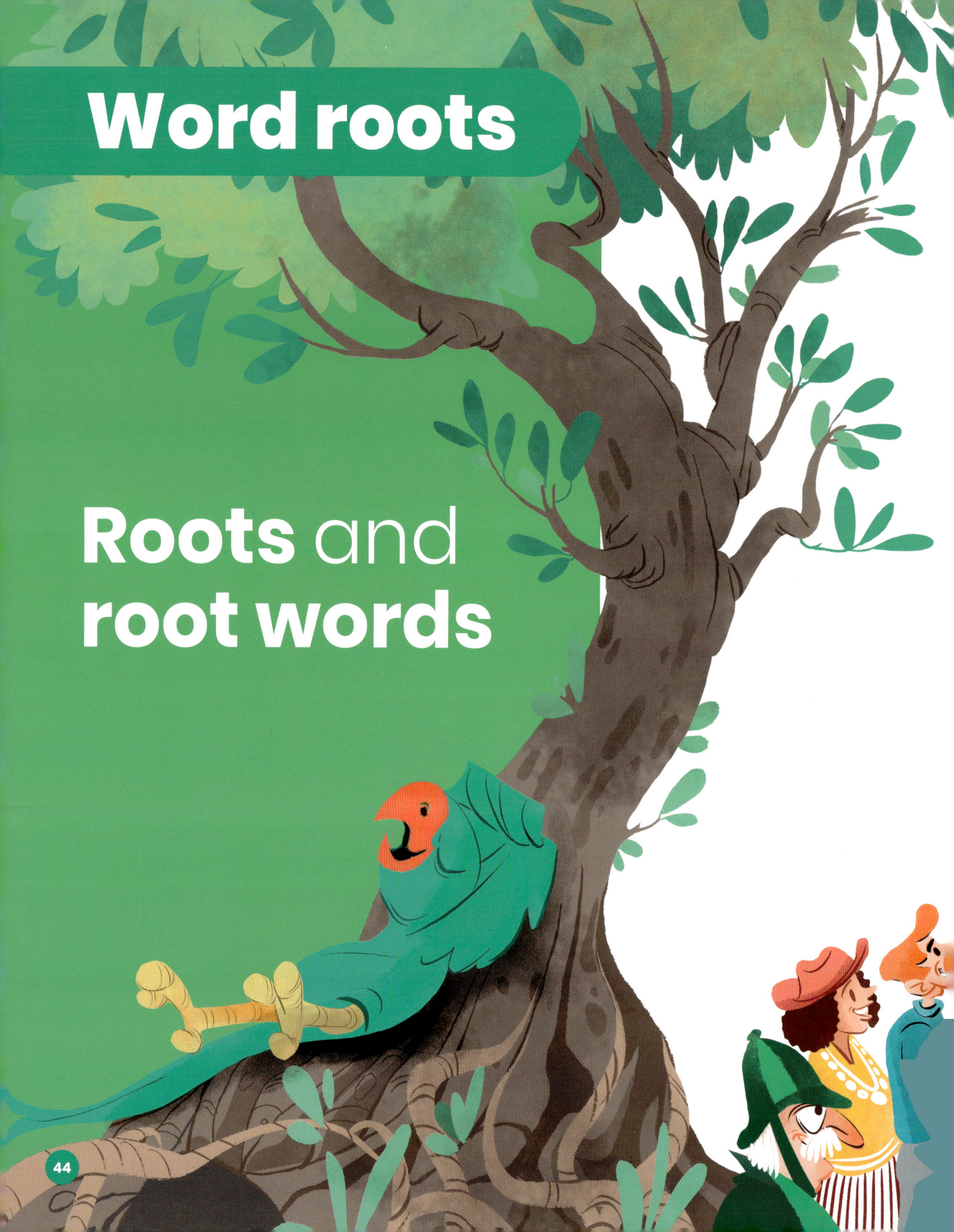

Word roots

Roots and root words

LATIN ORIGIN

audi

Meaning: **hearing, listening, or sound**

audi is a root used in many different words. It's like a magnet, pulling prefixes and suffixes to it to make new words, but all with similar meanings.

audiovisual

audio + visual (sight)
Literal meaning: both sound and sight

involving both sound and sight

audience

audi + ence (makes a noun)
Literal meaning: name of those hearing or listening

the group of people watching or listening to a play, concert, film, or public meeting

audition

audi + tion (makes a noun)
Literal meaning: power of hearing

a short performance given by an actor, dancer, musician, or other performer that tests whether that person's skills are suitable for a role

audiobook

audio + book
Literal meaning: sound book

a recorded reading of a book that you can listen to

Other words to learn:
audible
able to be heard

audiology
the science of hearing

audio
sound

audit
to examine and check

auditorium
a room where people listen

plaudit
praise or approval

FUN FACT!
The first audiobooks were created by The American Foundation for the Blind around 1932. They could be no more than 30 minutes long.

bio

Meaning: **life or living matter**

bio is a root word especially used in science compound words to describe things to do with the life of animals and plants.

biography

bio + graph/y (writing or recording)
Literal meaning: life in writing

an account of someone's life written by someone else

biosphere

bio + sphere (globe or ball)
Literal meaning: life, globe, or ball

Earth and all its living organisms

biology

bio + logy (science or study of)
Literal meaning: life or living matter science

scientific study of the natural processes of living things

aero**bic**

aero (air) + bio + ic (having to do with)
Literal meaning: having to do with air and life

able to live, grow, or take place only where there is oxygen

Other words to learn:

anaerobic
not needing oxygen to live

biographer
a person who writes an account of someone else's life

biodiversity
the number and types of plants and animals in a place or the world

biologist
a person who studies the natural processes of living things

symbiosis
when two animals or plants depend upon each other to live

antibiotic
a medicine that can destroy harmful bacteria in the body

FUN FACT!

A book about someone else's life is a biography, but a book about your own life is an autobiography. Auto means "self".

dict

LATIN ORIGIN

Meaning: **speak**

dict can appear at the beginning of a word, like "dictate", or at the end of a word, like "predict". It needs prefixes and suffixes to make sense as a whole word.

dictate

dict + ate (makes a verb)
Literal meaning: to speak

to say or read something for someone else to write down

diction

dict + ion (suggests action)
Literal meaning: speak with action

careful pronunciation of words in speech or singing

ver**dict**

ver (true) + dict
Literal meaning: true speak

an opinion or decision made after judging the information given, especially one made at the end of a trial in a court of law when deciding whether a person is guilty of a crime

dictionary

dic + tion + ary (makes a noun)
Literal meaning: a collection of words and phrases (dictionarium in Latin)

a book of alphabetically listed words, with definitions, etymologies, pronunciations and other information

CHALLENGE!

Dictate has many meanings. The meaning above is a verb, but it can be a noun, too. What do you think the noun "predicament" means?

———

an unpleasant situation that is difficult to get out of

Other words to learn:

contradict
to say the opposite of what someone else has said

dictatorship
a country ruled by a leader who has not been elected by the people

indication
a sign of something about to happen

dictum
a short statement, usually giving advice or stating a rule

dedicate
to give total energy, time, and focus to something

predict
to say that something will happen in the future

duc/duct

Meaning: **lead**

duc or **duct** features in many words, so let me introduce you to a few to "lead" you further in your education!

FUN FACT!
Pontcysyllte Aqueduct in Wales is the world's tallest navigable canal aqueduct at 38.4 m tall (126 ft).

e**duc**ate

e + duc + ate
Literal meaning: lead forth

to share knowledge and skills through formal instruction

re**duc**e

re (back) + duce
Literal meaning: lead back

to make something smaller in size, amount, or importance

con**duct**or

con + duct + or
Literal meaning: one who leads or guides

a person who directs a musical performance in front of an orchestra

aque**duct**

aque + duct
Literal meaning: water leading

a bridge that carries water over land

Other words to learn:

abduct
to take someone away by force

conduct
how someone acts or behaves

produce
to make something

deduce
to work out a fact or conclusion by reasoning

introduction
the first time or first part of something

viaduct
a type of bridge for traffic over a valley

fact

Meaning: **to make or do**

facts tell us about things that have already been done or established. Something factual is something to rely upon. We may use the expression "as a matter of fact" when discussing an issue with others.

arte**fact**

arte (skill) + fact
Literal meaning: skill made or a thing made by skill

something that is made by human art, especially if it is of historic or cultural interest

factory

fact + ory
Literal meaning: office for doers or makers

a large building where machines are used to make things

manu**fact**ure

manu (hand) + fact + ure
Literal meaning: to hand make something

to make large quantities of things in a factory

satis**fact**ion

satis + fact + ion
Literal meaning: to do enough

a happy or pleasant feeling

DID YOU KNOW?

fect as in "infect" and fic as in "fiction" have similar roots and meanings to "fact": to make or do. So it's useful to know your facts about fact, fect and fic!

Other words to learn:

benefactor
someone who helps others by giving money

significant
important

factor
a situation or fact that affects the result of something

factual
using facts to report something

magnificent
very beautiful or amazing

difficulty
the state of being hard to do, deal with, or understand

FUN FACT!

It is estimated that there are over three million industrial robots in use worldwide, helping to manufacture things.

fer

Meaning: **to bear, bring, or carry**

fer is a root used in many different words. Its words all have similar meanings related to bearing, bringing, or carrying, but this does not always mean just in the sense of transport.

ferry

fer + ry
Literal meaning: a passage over a river

a boat used to transport people and sometimes vehicles across water

con**fer**

con (together) + fer
Literal meaning: to bear together

to discuss in order to decide

trans**fer**

trans (across) + fer
Literal meaning: to carry across

to move things from one place to another

dif**fer**ence

dif (away from) + fer + ence (makes a noun)
Literal meaning: carry away from

the way in which two or more things are not the same

Other words to learn:

conference
an event where people meet to talk about a particular subject

defer
to delay something until later

differ
to be unlike something or someone else

infer
to guess something is true based on information you have

prefer
to like one thing better than another

suffer
to have pain

FUN FACT!

The fastest ferry in the world is a jet-powered catamaran ferry that crosses 225 km (140 miles) between Buenos Aires, Argentina, and Montevideo, Uruguay. It can transfer 1,024 passengers and 150 cars.

form

Meaning: **shape**

form is a root that "shapes" many other words, which in turn shape our thinking. The root can appear at the beginning, middle, or end of a word.

uni**form**

uni (one) + form
Literal meaning: one shape

a particular set of clothes that groups of people, like firefighters, are required to wear for their job

in**form**ation

in + form (a) + tion (makes a noun)
Literal meaning: something in shape

facts and figures

formula

form + ula (small)
Literal meaning: little form or rule

a repeated rule for doing something successfully

trans**form**

trans + form
Literal meaning: across shape

to change or convert something into something else

FUN FACT!

The formula for making Coca-Cola® was a closely guarded secret for about 125 years, from its creation in 1892 until it was moved to the World of Coca-Cola in Atlanta, Georgia. The formula is now on display in an exhibit called "The Vault of the Secret Formula."

Other words to learn:

conform
to follow expected rules

perform
to do an action, usually for others

performance
the act of entertaining others

formal
serious

formation
the way something is made or the making of something into a particular thing or shape

deformed
not a normal shape

reform
to make something better by making corrections

fract/frag

Meaning: **to break into pieces**

fract or **frag** appear in words that are about "bits and pieces". If you are feeling "fragile", you may feel like you're about to break into pieces, and if you have a "fracture", it's because you have slightly broken a bone.

fraction

fract + ion (makes a noun)
Literal meaning: something broken or divided

the result of dividing one whole number by another; a part of a whole

fragment

frag + ment (makes a noun)
Literal meaning: a piece broken off

a small piece of something

fragile

frag + ile (ability)
Literal meaning: ability to break easily into pieces

easily damaged or broken

fracture

fract + ure (makes a noun)
Literal meaning: a break

a slight crack or break of something hard, such as a bone or china

FUN FACT!

Did you know that bubbles, spiders' webs, and glass are some of the most fragile things in the world?

Other words to learn:

suffrage
the right to vote in an election

fragility
a quality of being delicate or easy to break

fractional
only part of something whole

fractious
easily upset or annoyed

fracas
a noisy fight or argument

refraction
when a ray of light changes direction through glass, water, or air

GREEK ORIGIN

geo

Meaning: **earth, soil, or global**

geo is a root of Greek origin and appears in many words that have to do with Earth. You have likely learned about geography at school, and many words linked to this subject use this root.

geography

geo + graphy
Literal meaning: earth description

a study of all or any of the things on Earth's surface

geothermal

geo + thermal (heat)
Literal meaning: earth heat

relating to or using the heat inside Earth

geometric

geo + metric
Literal meaning: earth measurement

having to do with lines, angles, curves and shapes

geology

geo + logy
Literal meaning: earth study

the study of how Earth was formed

Other words to learn:

geographic
relating to the study of all or any of the things on Earth's surface

geographer
a person who studies any of the things on Earth's surface

geologist
a person who studies how Earth was formed

geometry
the mathematical study of lines, angles, curves and shapes

geophysics
the study of rocks that make up Earth

geosphere
the outer layer of Earth

DID YOU KNOW?
If your name is George, it means earth farmer or earth worker. Are you a "Farmer George"?

53

graph

Meaning: **writing, recording, or written**

graph is a root of Greek origin and appears at the beginning and end of many common words you may know. Do you enjoy reading "graphic novels" or practising your "autograph"?

auto**graph**

auto (self) + graph
Literal meaning: self-writing

the signature of a person, usually a famous person

biblio**graph**y

biblio (books) + graph (something written) + y
Literal meaning: the writing of books

a list of the books and articles used by someone to help them write a book

para**graph**

para + graph
Literal meaning: beside writing

a section of a piece of writing used to help structure the piece

graphics

graph + ics (related to)
Literal meaning: related to drawing

pictures in a video or computer game

Other words to learn:

calligraphy
beautiful handwriting done with a brush or special pen

choreography
a planned pattern of steps and movements, usually for a dance

graffiti
writing or art made on public surfaces without permission

graphic novel
a book that tells a story in picture panels like those in a comic strip

photography
the art of using a camera to produce pictures

seismograph
a machine that measures  the size and duration of earthquakes

DID YOU KNOW?

The sense of the word "paragraph" has shifted from meaning the mark beside a piece of writing to the thing itself. Now, a paragraph is usually indicated by beginning on a new line, and sometimes with the line indented.

ject

Meaning: **throw**

ject is a root of Latin origin and appears in the middle or at the end of words. So we see "projector" and "object", but never a word beginning with *ject*. Many prefixes work well with *ject*.

pro**ject**

pro + ject
Literal meaning: forwards throw

to throw forwards

e**ject**

e (from ex) + ject
Literal meaning: out throw

to force out

inter**ject**

inter + ject
Literal meaning: to throw between

to say something that interrupts someone else

in**ject**ion

in + ject + ion
Literal meaning: in throw or a throwing in

a medicine put into the body with a syringe

CHALLENGE!
Try placing these prefixes in front of ject to make lots of words you may know already: *pro*; *ob*; *sub*; *re*; and *e*.

DID YOU KNOW?
"Project" as a noun, as in a "school project", has a similar meaning to the verb, because as we "plan, draft, or design", we are putting our ideas out there to explore. So a school project is a way for you to put your ideas forwards for others or for yourself.

Other words to learn:

conjecture
to guess based on limited information

object
to disagree with something (verb)

a fixed thing that you can touch or see, but that is not living (noun)

projector
a machine that projects images onto a screen or wall

subject
an area of knowledge or study at school (noun)

the thing or person that is the focus (noun)

to make someone do something unpleasant (verb)

trajectory
the path of a moving object

55

GREEK ORIGIN

morph

Meaning: **shape**

morph is a Greek root relating to shape. It literally "morphs" its way through different prefixes and suffixes to create a shape-shifting list of words.

meta**morph**osis

meta (change) + morph + osis (process)
Literal meaning: change shape process or the process of changing shape

a transformation of one thing into a different thing

morpheme

morph + eme (unit, sound)
Literal meaning: shape sound

the smallest unit of meaning in language that might include root, suffix, prefix

morphology

morph + ology (science or study of)
Literal meaning: study of shape, form

the study of the form of words and phrases

morph

morph
Literal meaning: to form or shape

to change in appearance and character

Other words to learn:

amorphous
having no fixed shape

anthropomorphic
human-shaped

bimorph
having two forms

morphing
changing shape or form

polymorph
having many shapes

FUN FACT!

In Greek mythology, Morpheus is the Greek god of dreams. Morpheus formed and shaped the dreams of those sleeping, even the dreams of gods and kings.

CHALLENGE!

Do you remember what the Latin root is for "shape"? Hint: you may have read about this on page 51.

form

neg

Meaning: **to say not or no**

neg is a Latin root relating to negativity or saying, "No!" It usually appears at the beginning of words. It can be spelled *ni* in the middle of words, and *ny* at the end.

negative

neg + ative (relating to)
Literal meaning: not relating or relating to saying no

considering only the bad aspects of a situation

neglect

neg + lect (pick up)
Literal meaning: to not pick up

to fail to take care of someone or something

negotiate

neg + otiate (ease)
Literal meaning: not with ease

to talk with others about a problem to solve it

de**ny**

de (completely) + ny
Literal meaning: completely not

to say something is not true

Other words to learn:

denial
to refuse to accept or give

negate
to make something ineffective

negativity
a state of being critical or gloomy

negligible
too small to be of any importance

negotiation
a process aimed at reaching an agreement

renege
to break a promise or an agreement

DID YOU KNOW?

Add the prefix *re* to negotiate and you get "renegotiate", which means to negotiate again. Add the prefix *non* and the suffix *able* and you get "nonnegotiable", which means there is no way to negotiate. What are your teacher's nonnegotiables?

phon/phone

Meaning: **sound**

phon or **phone** is a Greek root relating to sound. It appears in many words that are linked to communication since many of us rely on sound when speaking and listening.

micro**phone**

micro (small) + phone
Literal meaning: small sound

equipment that records small sounds and makes them louder

phoneme

phon + eme
Literal meaning: sound unit

a letter sound or group of sounds as represented by letter shapes (graphemes)

tele**phone**

tele (far) + phone
Literal meaning: far sound

a device used for speaking to someone who is not next to you

homo**phone**

homo (same) + phone
Literal meaning: same sound

words pronounced the same way but with a different meaning or spelling, like "two" and "too"

Other words to learn:

cacophony
an unpleasant, loud mix of sounds

headphones
speakers for the ears to listen to something without others hearing it

xylophone
a musical instrument that has wooden bars of different lengths, set in a row, and that each make a different sound when hit with a small mallet or hammer

phonetic
relating to speech sounds and the signs we use to represent them

phonics
a way to teach reading based on understanding how letter sounds and letter shapes work together in a language

saxophone
a metal musical instrument that makes sounds when the player blows into it through a very thin piece of wood called a reed

DID YOU KNOW?

Homographs are the opposite of homophones. They are words that are spelled the same but have a different meaning and may need to be pronounced differently. For example, "bow" (pronounced to rhyme with "low"), as in a "bow tie", and "bow" (pronounced to rhyme with "cow"), as in "the front of a ship".

GREEK ORIGIN

photo

Meaning: **light**

photo is a Greek root relating to light. It appears in many words that are linked to visual communication since we rely on light to make images.

photon

photo + (o)n
Literal meaning: light unit

a tiny particle of light

photograph

photo + graph (writing, written)
Literal meaning: light written

a picture taken with a camera

photosynthesis

photo + syn (together) + thesis (set, put)
Literal meaning: put light together

the process by which a plant uses the energy from the light of the sun to make its own food

photogenic

photo + genic (produced)
Literal meaning: light produced

able to look good in photographs without much effort

Other words to learn:

photocopier
a machine that uses light and electricity to make photographs or copies of documents and prints them

photocopy
a copy of a document produced using light and electricity

photographic
relating to the taking of pictures using a camera

photojournalist
a person who creates news stories, mainly using photographs

photosensitive
reactive to light

FUN FACT!
The world record for the most selfies was set in India in 2023: 184 pictures were taken in 3 minutes.

port

Meaning: **carry or harbour**

port has Latin origins. It appears in many words that are linked to things on the move because it is all about carrying.

portable

port + able
Literal meaning: able to be carried

something that can be carried

DID YOU KNOW?

"Portmanteau" is a French word that is used in English, too. It is a large travelling case, usually for clothes. We know that "port" means "carry" and "manteau" means "cloak or coat".

CHALLENGE!

"Portmanteau" can also mean blending two words together to combine their meanings. So, "ginormous" is a portmanteau of "gigantic" and "enormous". What is the portmanteau made from "breakfast" and "lunch"?

brunch

trans**port**

trans (across) + port
Literal meaning: carry across

to move people or things from one place to another

op**port**unity

op (in front of, towards) + port + unity (state of)
Literal meaning: coming towards a harbour

a situation that makes it possible to do something

porter

port + er
Literal meaning: person who carries

someone who carries luggage for others

Other words to learn:

export
to send goods to another country so they can be used, sold, or processed

import
to bring goods into a country so they can be used, sold, or processed

important
having great value or effect

portfolio
a personal collection of work or experience designed to impress others

report
to give a description of something or someone in a formal way

passport
an official document proving who a person is and that allows them to travel to other countries

pos/pon

Meaning: **place or put**

pos and **pon** arise from a Latin verb, *ponere*, meaning to "put or place". You see *pos* in a word like "compose". You see *pon* in a word like "opponent", but they all come from the same verb.

FUN FACT!

There are many famous musical composers. Beethoven composed some of his greatest musical pieces while deaf, and Mozart started composing at the age of five.

Other words to learn:

compose
to create music, formal writing, or poetry

depose
to remove a leader from power

juxtaposition
putting things that are not at all similar side by side

opponent
someone who disagrees with something and tries to change it

superimpose
to put an image on top of another so that both can still be seen

purpose
a reason for doing something

posture
the way someone holds their neck, back, and shoulders, usually when standing or sitting, but also in dance

dis**pos**al

dis + pos + al
Literal meaning: set apart

the act of getting rid of something you no longer need or want

post**pone**

post (after) + pon(e)
Literal meaning: after place or to place after

to delay a plan that was in place

position

pos(i) + tion
Literal meaning: the act of placing

to put something in place

sup**pose**

sup (under) + pos(e)
Literal meaning: put under

to think that something is likely to be true

DID YOU KNOW?

Sometimes "position" also has the meaning of a person's status, such as, "She had a very important position in the theatre".

61

rupt

Meaning: **burst, break**

rupt has Latin roots and helps us understand a whole set of words that are about bursting out and breaking. If you think of words bursting out of an erupting volcano, you may remember its meaning!

dis**rupt**ion

dis (apart) + rupt + ion (makes a noun)
Literal meaning: the bursting apart of something

the act of preventing something from happening

inter**rupt**

inter (between) + rupt
Literal meaning: between bursts

to do or say something that stops someone else from their speech or action

e**rupt**

e (out) + rupt
Literal meaning: to break out

to burst in an unexpected way

rupture

rupt + ure (outcome or result)
Literal meaning: burst result

to tear or split open

Other words to learn:

abrupt
unexpected and sudden

bankrupt
having no money or being unable to pay what you owe

corrupt
getting an advantage by being dishonest

incorruptible
unable to be enticed to do anything that is morally wrong

disrupt
to stop something from happening in its normal way

eruption
when something bursts out or explodes

interruption
when something or someone stops something for a short time

FUN FACT!

A volcano is literally an open hole in the Earth's surface out of which burst gases, ash and hot liquid rock, known as magma, when it erupts. There are volcanoes under the sea, too, and they sometimes form islands.

GREEK ORIGIN

scope

Meaning: **see, examine, view, or observe**

You'll know lots of words that use the Greek root **scope**, often linked to equipment that helps us to view things more clearly or in a different way. This is a useful root for scientists.

micro**scope**

micro (small) + scope
Literal meaning: small examine

a device that makes very small things look bigger

tele**scope**

tele (far) + scope
Literal meaning: far view

a device for making things that are far away look closer and larger

peri**scope**

peri (around) + scope
Literal meaning: around view

a long vertical tube that gives a view of what is above you when you can't just look up to see

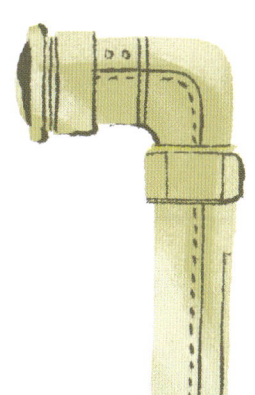

stetho**scope**

stetho (chest) + scope
Literal meaning: chest view

a piece of medical equipment that doctors use to listen to your heart and lungs

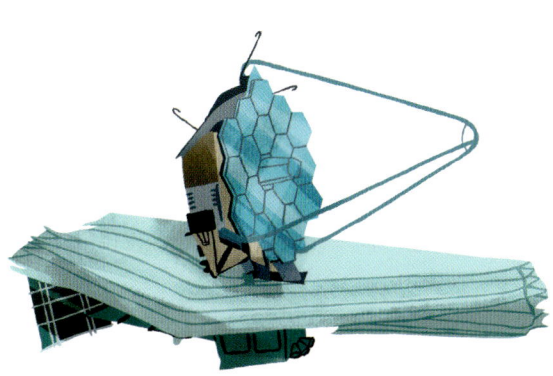

Other words to learn:

gyroscope
a device for keeping things horizontal, also used as a toy

horoscope
information about what might happen to you, based on when you were born in relation to the stars and planets

kaleidoscope
a tube that you look through to see patterns of light made by coloured glass and mirrors

microscopic
very tiny

scope
the range of something

telescopic
able to see things far away

FUN FACT!

The largest space telescope is the James Webb Space Telescope, which was launched in December 2021. Its mirror has a diameter of 6.5 m (more than 20 ft).

scrib/script

Meaning: **write or written**

scrib or **script** is a Latin root from the verb "scribere" (now you know some Latin!), that is widely used in words about writing. A scribe is someone who writes, and "scribe" is also a verb meaning "to write".

Other words to learn:

descriptive
tells how something looks in an interesting and detailed way

description
information that tells what someone or something is like

inscription
words that are cut or written into something else, like stone

prescribe
to give an instruction about or to make a rule for others

scribe
to write

script
the words that will be spoken in a play or film

transcribe
to write down something that is spoken or played

de**scribe**

de (out, down) + scribe
Literal meaning: to write out or down

to say or write what something is like in words

manu**script**

manu + write
Literal meaning: hand write

the words of a book before it is printed

scribble

scrib + ble
Literal meaning: marks made hastily

quick or careless written marks

pre**script**ion

pre (before) + script + ion (makes a noun)
Literal meaning: a writing before

an order from a doctor with details of the medicine or drugs that someone needs

DID YOU KNOW?
P.S. is short for "postscript". And a postscript is when you want to add a note to the end of a piece of writing. P.S. It means "to write after".

sist

Meaning: **stand, make, or be firm**

sist is a Latin root that is usually at the end of a word, which means it attracts prefixes, like "consist". It particularly attracts *per*, *in*, *re* and *sub*, to name a few.

insist

in + sist
Literal meaning: in taking a stand

to say firmly even if others disagree

persist

per + sist
Literal meaning: thoroughly firm

to continue in spite of difficulty or opposition

resist

re + sist
Literal meaning: against a stand

to refuse to accept

assistant

as + sist + ant
Literal meaning: a person who stands by

someone who helps

Other words to learn:

ecstatic
extremely happy

consistent
not changing

desist
to stop doing something

exist
to be or to live

irresistible
too good to refuse

subsist
to have just enough food or money to live

substitute
to use a thing or person in place of another

stationary
not moving or changing

DID YOU KNOW?

In another ancient language called Proto-Indo-European, sta is a root with the same meaning as sist. It means "to stand, make, or be firm" and appears in words such as "stand" and "stare". So, sist and sta are quite close, and so are stat and stit!

CHALLENGE!

Complete this word sum. What is this word?
ir (prefix) + **re** (prefix) + **sist** (root) + **ible** (suffix) = **?**

___
irresistible

spect

Meaning: see, look

spect often appears when the meaning has something to do with seeing or looking. You may need to put on your spectacles to inspect and make sure!

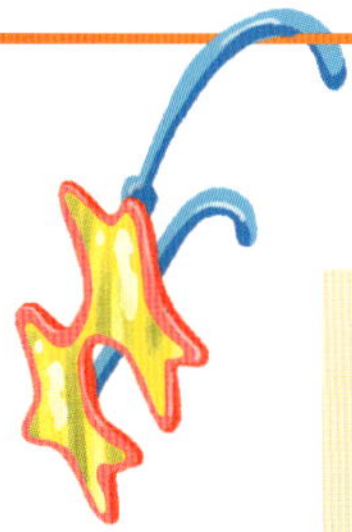

in**spect**

in + spect
Literal meaning: in taking a look

to look carefully or closely

spectator

spect + ator (makes a noun)
Literal meaning: a watcher or viewer

someone who watches an event

spectacles

spect + acles
Literal meaning: name of things for seeing

eyewear, glasses

per**spect**ive

per (forwards, through) + spect + ive (causing, or making)
Literal meaning: look through

a particular way of seeing or thinking about something

Other words to learn:

circumspect
careful to avoid risks

inspector
someone who looks at something very carefully to make sure it is correct

prospect
the possibility of something happening

retrospective
looking back in time

spectacular
especially good or exciting to look at

special
unusual, often in a good way

species
a set of animals or plants that have similar characteristics and can breed with each other

suspect
to think something is likely to be true

FUN FACT!

The world record for the largest number of spectators at an American football game was set in 2016. There were 130,045 people.

CHALLENGE!

Can you remember the Greek root with the same meaning as spect? Hint: look at page 63.

scope

str/struct

Meaning: **activity or to build**

str and **struct** are roots of Latin origin and will be sure to make you think of the word "structure". We all need structure in our lives and to work industriously!

indu**str**y

indu (active) + str + y
Literal meaning: actively make or build something

a business that produces goods for sale, often in a factory

in**struct**ion

in + struct + ion
Literal meaning: to pile in or on

an order to do something or an explanation of how to do something

ob**struct**ion

ob (in the way of) + struct + ion
Literal meaning: in the way of building

something that blocks so no progress can be made

de**struct**ion

de + struct + ion
Literal meaning: unbuild

ruining something

Other words to learn:

construction
the process of building

indestructible
impossible to break

infrastructure
the basic services and systems that a country or organisation uses to make sure things work as they should and people have what they need

instructor
someone who tells others what to do

instrument
a tool that is used to do a particular job or is played to make music

structure
the organisation or arrangement of something that is made or built

unstructured
not clearly organised or arranged

FUN FACT!

Nothing on earth is truly "indestructible", but a tiny eight-legged micro-animal is thought to be as close to indestructible as it gets: the tardigrade. It is able to live for up to 30 years without food or water and can survive extreme temperatures, deep sea and space.

ten/tain/tin

Meaning: **hold or stretch**

ten, **tain** and **tin** all relate to the Latin verb meaning "to hold".
They form a very long list of words.

DID YOU KNOW?

You may know the phrase, "to be on tenterhooks", which you use when you are feeling stressed about awaiting news. A tenter was a wooden frame used to stretch cloth in the 1300s. The "hook" refers to one of the hooks that held the cloth on the frame. So if you feel like you are "on tenterhooks", it's like saying you feel painfully stretched like a very tight piece of cloth in the 1300s. Ouch!

de**ten**tion

de (away, from) + ten + tion
Literal meaning: hold away from

making someone stay in a place, especially as a punishment

enter**tain**

enter (inter/among) + tain
Literal meaning: hold among

to provide interesting or enjoyable things to watch or do

con**tain**er

con (together) + tain + er
Literal meaning: holds together

something that holds something else

con**tin**ue

con (together) + tin + ue
Literal meaning: join together so uninterrupted

to carry on

Other words to learn:

contentment
satisfaction with a situation

detain
to hold someone or something in a place by force

discontentment
unhappiness or dissatisfaction with a situation

entertainment
interesting and enjoyable things for people to watch or do

maintain
to keep or continue at the same level

retain
to keep

tenacious
not willing to give up

tenant
someone who pays money for the use of land or a building, including a house

tele

Meaning: **far, distant, or complete**

tele is of Greek origin. You will recognise many of the words it creates, like "television" and "telephone". You may be less familiar with the word "telepathy", which means "feeling from afar".

FUN FACT!

"Television" is quite a new word because the first televisions were not fully developed until about 1907. When the first televisions were in development, other possible names were considered alongside "television", including "telephote" and "televista".

television

tele + vision (sight)
Literal meaning: far sight

a technology system with a screen that shows moving images and sounds

telephone

tele + phone (sound)
Literal meaning: far sound

a device used for speaking to someone who is not next to you

telescope

tele + scope (view)
Literal meaning: far view

a device for making things that are far away look closer and larger

telekinesis

tele + kinesis (movement)
Literal meaning: far movement

the movement of objects using the power of the mind, without making physical contact with them

Other words to learn:

telecommunications
the sending and receiving of messages using electronic devices

telegram
an old-fashioned way of sending messages by electrical or radio signals

telepathy
the communication of what is in your mind with someone else without speaking

teleport
the fictional action of moving something across a distance instantaneously

telescopic
able to see things far away

telethon
an extended television programme or campaign that collects money for a charity from its viewers

tract

Meaning: **pull or drag**

tract is a root used in many different words. It's like a magnet pulling prefixes and suffixes to it to make new words!

con**tract**

con (together) + tract
Literal meaning: pull together

a legal agreement between two or more people or groups

ex**tract**

ex (out) + tract
Literal meaning: pull out

to remove or take something out

tractor

tract + or (that which)
Literal meaning: that which pulls

a motor vehicle with large back wheels and thick tyres, used on farms for pulling machinery

dis**tract**

dis (apart/away) + tract
Literal meaning: draw away from

to draw attention away from one thing and towards something else

FUN FACT!

In December 2023, Shohei Ohtani, the major league basketball star, signed a record 10-year contract worth $700 million with the Los Angeles Dodgers, which means he is one of the highest paid athletes in the world.

Other words to learn:

abstract
general, not specific

attract
to pull towards something or someone else

attraction
a quality that makes something or someone interesting and appealing

retract
to pull something back in or to take back something that was said

subtract
to take one number from another number

traction
the friction between a thing and the surface it's moving over

LATIN ORIGIN

vert

Meaning: **turn**

vert is a root used to create words with a shared meaning to do with "turning". We turn to a new topic in conversation, or when we see a detour sign on a journey.

ROAD CLOSED

re**ver**se

re + ver(s) + e
Literal meaning: to turn around

to change something to its opposite

di**ver**sion

di (from) + ver(s) + ion
Literal meaning: a turning from

a thing or action intended to make someone or something turn in a different direction

extro**vert**

extr(a) + (out) + vert
Literal meaning: one who turns out

an outgoing person who seeks out social interactions

con**ver**sation

con (with, together) + ver(s) + ation (action)
Literal meaning: to turn about with

talking with someone, usually informally

Other words to learn:

adverse
actions that are unfavourable for you

convert
to change into a different form

divert
to make something or someone follow a different route

transverse
something that is turned crosswise or diagonally

universal
something that applies to everyone in the world or in a group

versatile
someone who has many skills or something that has many uses

CHALLENGE!
Do you think you are an extrovert or an introvert (someone who is energised by spending time alone rather than with others)? Why? What about your best friend?

DID YOU KNOW?
A long time ago, around 1350, "conversation" had a different meaning that was more about your way of life, where and how you lived. Only later in history, did it have the meaning we understand today, linking it to informal talking.

vis / vid

Meaning: **see**

vis/vid is a root linked to seeing. Sometimes we see the letters *vis* as in "vision" and sometimes *vid* as in "evidence".

e**vid**ence

e (fully) + vid + ence
Literal meaning: fully see

facts or information that prove something is true

in**vis**ible

in + vis + ible
Literal meaning: not seen

something that cannot be seen by the eye

vision

vis + ion
Literal meaning: act of seeing

the sense of seeing

visitor

vis + it + or (makes a noun)
Literal meaning: person who sees

someone who visits a place or person

Other words to learn:

envision
to imagine something

revise
to change something, often to improve it

supervision
direction or control of people or animals

televise
to broadcast an event or programme on television

video
a film, event, or action recorded digitally and available to watch online

visible
able to be seen

visor
part of a hat or helmet that can be pulled down to protect a person's face or eyes

vista
a view, often from a high place

FUN FACT!

In the Harry Potter books, an Invisibility Cloak is handed down from generation to generation in Harry's family. Harry isn't sure at first of its true powers, and he mainly uses it to move around Hogwarts both inside and outside, so as not to be seen. How would you use a cloak that could make you "invisible"?

LATIN ORIGIN

vor

Meaning: **eat**

vor is a root linked to eating, and it tends to create quite long words. But don't worry, they are easy to understand once you use your morphology skills to split them up into smaller units!

insecti**vor**e

insect + vor(e)
Literal meaning: insect-eating

an animal or plant that eats insects

carni**vor**e

carni + vor(e)
Literal meaning: meat-eating

an animal that eats meat

FUN FACT!

Some examples of insectivores include different kinds of frogs, lizards, bats and spiders. A spider catching a bug in a web is an example of the way an insectivore acts to catch its food.

herbi**vor**e

herbi + vor(e)
Literal meaning: plant-eating

an animal that eats plants

omni**vor**e

omni (all) + vor(e)
Literal meaning: eating all

an animal that eats meat and plants

Other words to learn:

carnivorous
meat-eating

devour
to eat up greedily

herbivorous
plant-eating

insectivorous
insect-eating

omnivorous
eating anything

voracious
eating a large quantity of food greedily

Prefixes

Relating to negativity

Relating to time

Relating to direction or position

Relating to size or amount

a/an

Meaning: **not, without**

a or **an** can be used to change the meaning of a word or root into a negative meaning. But not all words beginning with *a/an* are negative; in some Old English words such as "asleep" or "ashore" the *a/an* prefix means "in or on".

abyss

a + byss (bottom)
Literal meaning: without a bottom, bottomless

a very deep hole in the Earth or sea

anaemic

an + aemic (blood)
Literal meaning: without blood

pale, sickly looking, or weak

anonymous

an + onymous (name)
Literal meaning: without a name

no name known or acknowledged

amnesia

a + mnesia (remember)
Literal meaning: not remembering

loss of memory, usually because of a head injury or illness

Other words to learn:

alopecia
loss of hair

acentric
having no centre

adamant
impossible to persuade or change

anaemia
a condition in which there is a lack of red blood cells

anarchy
no government

apathetic
not caring/without feeling

DID YOU KNOW?
"Anon" is the shortened version or abbreviation of the word "anonymous". Some nursery rhymes and poems are anon, because we just can't be sure who first wrote them.

GREEK ORIGIN

anti

Meaning: **against, opposite**

anti is a prefix used to change a word or root word to have a negative or opposite meaning. So "antifreeze" is the opposite of "freeze".

antisocial

anti + social
Literal meaning: against friends

unfriendly to others or society

antifreeze

anti + freeze
Literal meaning: against freezing

a liquid added to cooling water to prevent it from freezing

antibiotic

anti + biotic (living things)
Literal meaning: against living things

medicine that can destroy harmful bacteria in the body

antiseptic

anti + septic (infected)
Literal meaning: against infection

something that kills germs and harmful bacteria

FUN FACT!

The first antibiotic was called penicillin and was discovered on mould in a forgotten petri dish by the scientist Alexander Fleming in 1928. He called it "mould juice".

Other words to learn:

Antarctic
opposite to the Arctic

antidote
a way of preventing something bad

antigravity
opposite effect of gravity

antiperspirant
helps reduce sweating

antibullying
against bullying

antithesis
opposite idea/thing

LATIN ORIGIN

contra

Meaning: **against, opposite**

contra, **contro** and **counter** have similar meanings to *anti*, but we have to learn when to use each. We can't just say "antidict" instead of "contradict", or "counterversy" instead of "controversy".

Other words to learn:

contrast
to look at the way two or more things are different

contraband
goods that are taken in or out of a country illegally

contravene
to break a rule

control
to limit or order something or someone

counterculture
ideas and values that are completely different from those of the rest of society

controversial
causing disagreement; disputable

contrary

contra + ry (makes a noun)
Literal meaning: opposite, opposed

an idea, attitude, or reaction that is completely different from or opposite to another

counterfeit

counter + feit
Literal meaning: something made against something else

fake but made to look genuine

contradict

contra + dict (say)
Literal meaning: speak the opposite

to say the opposite of what someone else has said

controversy

contro + vers (turn) + y
Literal meaning: turned against

a lot of disagreement or argument about something

FUN FACT!

In Türkiye and China, as long ago as 600 BCE, the method used to counterfeit coins was to mix in other less expensive metals with gold and silver. Other methods of counterfeiting were to cover a coin made out of less expensive metal with a thin gold coating, or to clip tiny pieces of a real coin, melt them, and make another coin from the pieces.

de

Meaning: **do the opposite of**

de is another prefix used to give a negative meaning to a word. So, you can "activate" something to make it start, and "deactivate" it to make it stop. It can also mean to reduce something or remove it.

deactivate

de + activ(e) + ate (makes a verb)
Literal meaning: don't put into action

to stop something from being active

decrease

de + crease (grow)
Literal meaning: to grow away from

to reduce

decide

de + cide (cut)
Literal meaning: to cut off

to choose after considering options

deceive

de + ceive (take)
Literal meaning: take from

to persuade someone that something false is the truth, or to keep the truth hidden for your own advantage

Other words to learn:

debug
to remove mistakes from a computer programme

deception
a trick you play on others for your own advantage

decision
a choice made after considering possibilities or options

defrost
to thaw so something is free of ice

de-emphasise
to play down or reduce

derail
to prevent something from continuing as planned

FUN FACT!

Imagine you are a king or queen. What might cause you to be dethroned? Well, you might just become less popular among your people, or they rise against you in a revolution. Or you might lose a war and have to step down because you failed. Or you might just decide you no longer want to do the job and choose to dethrone yourself, which is called abdication.

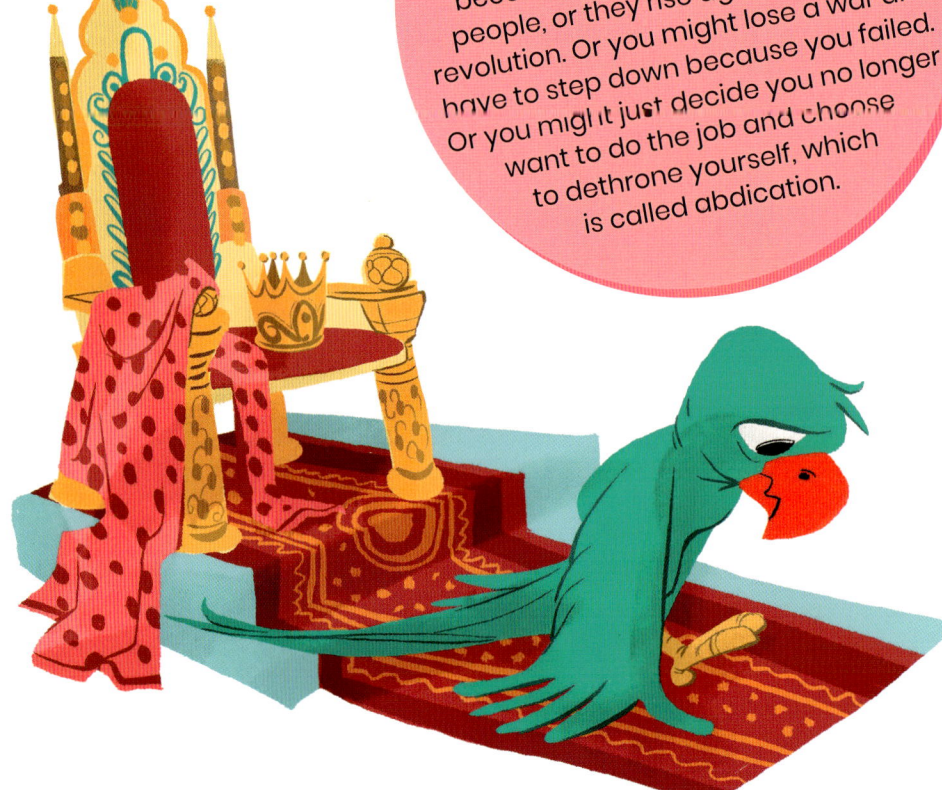

dif/dis

Meaning: **apart, away from, do the opposite of**

dif and **dis** therefore have a very similar meaning to *de* on the previous page.

dissect

dis + sect (cut)
Literal meaning: cut apart

to cut a dead body or plant open to study its structure

difference

dif + fer (to carry) + ence (makes a noun)
Literal meaning: to carry or set apart

a way in which two or more things are not the same

disappear

dis + appear
Literal meaning: not appear

to no longer be seen

discount

dis + count
Literal meaning: not count or matter

to not take into account

Other words to learn:
different
not alike or similar

digression
a straying or wandering

disappoint
to let down or sadden

dishonest
to lie or be deceitful

disobey
to resist or rebel against a rule

dissection
the act of cutting a dead body or plant open to study its structure

FUN FACT!

"Discount" can also mean to reduce the price of something in order to sell it faster. Sometimes we see "50% discount", and sometimes shops or online sites use fun acronyms like BOGOF, which means "Buy One, Get One Free."

il

Meaning: **not, without**

il is added to words that begin with the letter 'l' to make words with the opposite meaning. Prefixes with very similar meanings are *im*, *ir*, and *in*.

illicit

il + licit (lawful)
Literal meaning: not lawful

not allowed

illogical

il + logic (reason) + al (related to)
Literal meaning: not related to reason

not reasonable or practical; without sense

illegible

il + legible
Literal meaning: not readable

not readable; unreadable

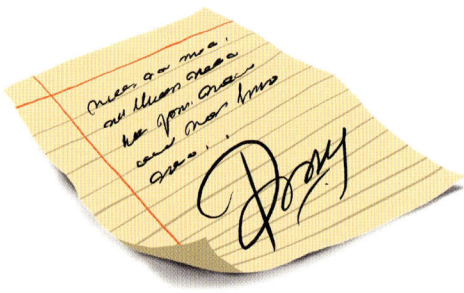

illegal

il + legal
Literal meaning: not legal

not allowed by law; unlawful

Other words to learn:

illiberal
small-minded or intolerant

illiterate
unable to read or write

illiteracy
lack of education

illogicality
not based on logic; not making sense

illegitimate
against the law

illusive
not real or true

DID YOU KNOW?

A note of caution: not all words beginning with "ill" are linked to the prefix *il*. In the word "illustrate", there is no negative meaning, as it originates from the Latin verb, "illustrare", which means "to light up, make light". Nowadays, we think of it meaning "to make pictures". The illustrations in this book are extraordinary!

im

Meaning: **not, without**

Guess what? **im** is also part of the prefix family that has a negative meaning, and is added to words that begin with 'm', 'p', or 'b' to form words with the opposite meaning.

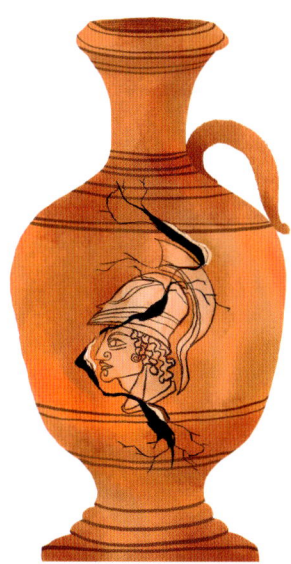

immature

im + mature (time, ripe)
(notice the double 'm')
Literal meaning: not timely or ripe

not yet matured; not acting one's age

DID YOU KNOW?

If you use "imperfect" as an adjective to describe something, ("It was an imperfect solution to a difficult problem." The stress is on the second syllable, "per". But if you use "imperfection" as a noun, ("There is an imperfection in that fabric."), the stress is on the third syllable, "fec".

imperfect

im + perfect (excellent, complete)
Literal meaning: not excellent or complete

damaged or having some problems

impossible

im + possible (can be done)
Literal meaning: cannot be done

cannot happen or be achieved

impatient

im + pati (suffer, endure) + ent (to be)
Literal meaning: cannot endure

easily annoyed by having to wait for something

CHALLENGE!

An American singer and songwriter once sang, "Act your age, not your shoe size," in one of his songs. What did he mean?

Act in a more mature way

Other words to learn:

imbalance
unevenness or unfairness

impartial
neutral or objective

impatience
restlessness or annoyance

immeasurable
unable to be measured

impolite
rude

improper
out of place or unsuitable

in

Meaning: **not, without**

It's incredible, but yes, **in** is another prefix that changes the meaning of a word to its opposite. It's just like *un*, *il*, *im* and *ir*.

inactive

in + active (doing)
Literal meaning: not doing

not moving or unable to move or work any more

LIKE THIS!

That computer is now inactive.

I've been unwell and inactive.

invisible

in + vis (to see) + ible (makes an adjective)
Literal meaning: cannot be seen

impossible to see

inappropriate

in + ap (to) + propri (own) + ate (makes an adjective)
Literal meaning: not make one's own

not suitable, especially for the time, place, or situation

DID YOU KNOW?

Do you know the difference between the words "flammable" and "inflammable"? Does one mean that it is easily set on fire and one mean the opposite? Think again! These two words have the exact same meaning. How confusing! This is because the prefix *in* can also be used to mean "in or into".

incorrect

in + correct (to put straight)
Literal meaning: not put straight

wrong or not true

Other words to learn:

incomplete
not finished

inexcusable
not forgivable

intolerant
narrow-minded about ideas that are different from your own

insipid
watered down, bland

independent
separate, self-supporting

invalid
having no legal power, untrue

ir

Meaning: **not, without, the opposite of**

ir is thought to be linked to the prefix *in*, which changes to *ir* before words beginning with 'r'. So instead of "inregular", we have "irregular".

irrelevant

ir + relevant
Literal meaning: not helpful

not connected with what is being discussed

irregular

ir + regular
Literal meaning: not having rules

not forming a regular pattern

irresponsible

ir + responsible
Literal meaning: not trustworthy

doing something without considering the possible outcomes; not taking care of things

irrational

ir + rational
Literal meaning: not sensible

without logical reason or common sense

LIKE THIS!

It's irrational, but I love the smell of popcorn.

My mum says I am irritating, but I say I am irresistible and it's irrefutable!

Other words to learn:

irrational number
a number that cannot be written as a fraction

irreconcilable
impossible to find agreement about

irrefutable
impossible to prove incorrect

irreplaceable
impossible to substitute

irresistible
impossible to avoid or refuse

irreversible
impossible to undo or go back

83

mis

Meaning: **bad, badly, wrong**

mis is added to some nouns and verbs to change their meaning to its opposite. It suggests that something is wrong or done badly, or that it's a mistake!

misadventure

mis + adventure (chance)
Literal meaning: bad chance

bad luck or an accident

miscalculate

mis + calcul + ate
Literal meaning: badly calculate

to make a mistake, especially in numbers or distance

misspell

mis + spell (notice the double 's')
Literal meaning: badly spell

to make a spelling mistake

mistake

mis + take
Literal meaning: badly take or take in error

to make an error

Other words to learn:

misbehave
to behave badly

misfortune
bad luck

mishear
to not hear correctly and mistake what was said

misinformation
false information

mislead
to deceive

misplace
to lose something knowing it can be found

FUN FACT!

We all make mistakes, but we can learn from them! If you reflect on your mistake, you can avoid repeating the same mistake. Make mistakes to learn!

LATIN ORIGIN

non

Meaning: **no, not, without**

non is a very useful prefix if we want to say what something is not. It is used in front of adjectives and nouns to form words that describe something as not having a particular feature or quality.

nonsense

non + sense (meaning)
Literal meaning: not meaningful

something that is silly or stupid

nonconformist

non + con (together) + form + ist (one who)
Literal meaning: someone who does not form or act in the same way as others

someone who lives and thinks in a different way from the majority of other people

DID YOU KNOW?

There are no hard and fast rules about when or whether to use a hyphen with a prefix such as *non*. A good general rule is to avoid a hyphen wherever possible, but if the prefix falls before a proper noun, use a hyphen (e.g. non-European).

Other words to learn:

nondescript
not able to be distinguished; ordinary

nonexistent
imaginary or not real

nonstarter
an idea or proposed action with no chance of success

nonstop
without stopping

nonchalant
not concerned or bothered

nonessential
not required

nondairy
made without animal milk

nonfiction

non + fiction (build, form)
Literal meaning: not a narrative story form

text that deals with facts or real events rather than made-up stories

nonstick

non + stick
Literal meaning: not sticky

preventing things from sticking

un

Meaning: **not, opposite to, lacking**

un is a common prefix for adjectives, adverbs and nouns when we want to form words that have the opposite meaning. It can also be added to the beginning of verbs to describe the reverse of a process.

FUN FACT!

A man called Frane Selak, born in Croatia in 1929, is said to have been the luckiest unlucky man to have ever lived. He survived accidents with most forms of transport and is said to have escaped death seven times. In telling his tales, he became a celebrity!

unusual

un + usual (ordinary)
Literal meaning: not ordinary

different from others of the same type

undecided

un + decid(e) (cut off) + ed (makes an adjective)
Literal meaning: not cut off

not sure about a decision

unhappy

un + happ (chance, luck) + y (full of)
Literal meaning: not full of luck

not pleased; sad

uncomfortable

un + comfort (to help, strengthen) + able (makes an adjective)
Literal meaning: not helping

not feeling pleasant; awkward

DID YOU KNOW?

In most European languages, the word "happy" at first meant "lucky", but the meaning changed over time to mean "very pleased".

Other words to learn:

unfortunate
caused by or causing bad luck

uninspired
not interesting or exciting

unknown
not familiar

unable
not having the ability, power or permission to do something

unrest
discontent, protest

unearth
to discover

unlock
to open with a key, code, or electronic device

LATIN ORIGIN

ante

Meaning: **before, in front**

ante is a prefix of Latin origin that is useful for creating compound words. Its Greek form is *anti*, but that also has the meaning of "against or the opposite of", so its use needs careful consideration.

antique

ant + ique (to see)
Literal meaning: seen before

made in an earlier period of time, often considered to be rare, beautiful, and of high value

antennae

ante + nnae (to stretch before)
Literal meaning: to stretch before

a pair of long feelers usually on the head of insects and crustaceans

antler

ant + ler
Literal meaning: horn in front of the eyes

a horn (like a branch) that grows on the head of reindeer, caribou, male deer (stags), and male moose (bulls)

anticipate

anti + cip (take) + ate (makes a verb)
Literal meaning: take before

to expect something will happen

Other words to learn:

antebellum
the period of time before the American Civil War

antechamber
an entrance hall or lobby

anterior
towards the front or at the front

anticipated
on the way or expected

anticipation
the sense of expecting something to happen

avant-garde
something that is ahead of its time

DID YOU KNOW?

"Antenna" is singular, meaning just one antenna, but this word is usually plural because there are usually two of them: "antennae". Another word that has this same *ae* plural ending is "formula" (formulae).

87

fore

Meaning: **in front of, before, earlier**

fore is a prefix used to create new words with the meaning of "in front of" or "before". Today, we use "before" as a word in its own right and with the same meaning.

foreboding

fore + bod (be aware) + ing
Literal meaning: aware of before

a feeling that something very bad is about to happen

forehead

fore + head
Literal meaning: before the head

the flat part of the face above the eyebrows

forefinger

fore + finger
Literal meaning: first before the thumb

the first, or index, finger

forecast

fore + cast (plan, prepare)
Literal meaning: to plan before

to predict

Other words to learn:

beforehand
earlier than a particular time

forebear
a relative from the past, also know as an ancestor

foresight
the ability to anticipate and plan for something in the future

foreman
a supervisor who directs other people working

foreword
an introductory statement at the front of a book

forwards
leading at or near the front

forehand
a stroke played in sports like tennis, in which the palm of the hand faces the direction in which you are hitting the ball

DID YOU KNOW?

Some words are homophones. They sound the same but have a different meaning and/or spelling. For example, the words "forwards" and "foreword". You can go forwards (towards the front), but you read a foreword (an introduction to a book).

CHALLENGE!

What do you call a person who forecasts?

A forecaster

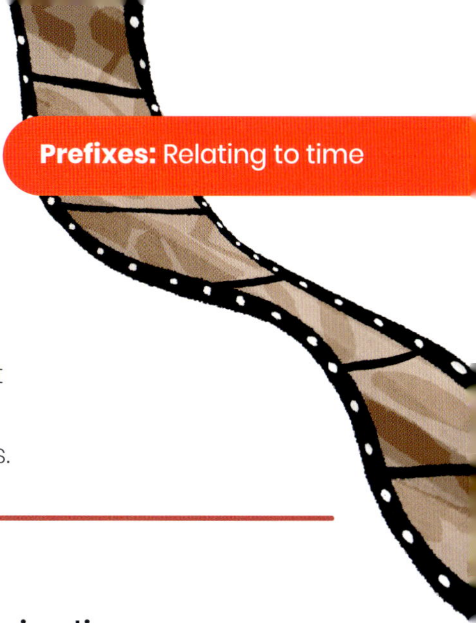

pre

Meaning: **in front of, before, earlier**

This is a preamble to prepare you for this list of words that use the prefix of Latin origin meaning "before". **pre** is very similar in meaning to *ante* and *fore* on the previous pages.

prepare

pre + pare
Literal meaning: to make ready

to get ready in advance

prepaid

pre + paid
Literal meaning: to pay before

paid in advance

premiere

pre + miere
Literal meaning: first performance

the first performance or showing of a film, play, or song

prejudice

pre + judice (judgment)
Literal meaning: before judgment

an unfair opinion or feeling, especially when formed without knowledge or through hatred

Other words to learn:

preamble
an introductory statement

precaution
an action taken in advance to safeguard or protect

preview
a taster or sample

pretend
to make believe

precursor
something that goes before

prebooked
arranged for the future

prediction
what you think may happen

premonition
a feeling that something is going to happen

FUN FACT!

The red-carpet tradition is thought to have originated in 1928 at the film premiere of *Robin Hood*. It was used to hide mud on the walkway, much as it does today when celebrities arrive in expensive footwear!

re

Meaning: **again**

re is a very useful prefix and will almost certainly be one you recognise. It is often attached to a verb and means to do something over again.

reappearance

re + appear (come into sight) + ance (makes a noun)
Literal meaning: come into sight again

a return of someone or something that has been gone

react

re + act
Literal meaning: act again(st)

to respond to something

reread

re + read
Literal meaning: read again

to read something again

rehearsal

re + hears (drag over) + al (makes a noun)
Literal meaning: go over again

a practice to prepare for a performance

Other words to learn:

redefine
to give something a new meaning

refine
to improve

rewrite
to improve something written by updating it

revival
the process of freshening something to make it popular again

relax
to become calm and less active

reiterate
to say something again for emphasis

respectful
showing admiration or respect for someone or something

repellant
something that keeps pests away

DID YOU KNOW?

Think about the two words, "recover" and "re-cover". The first you do after you've been unwell, while the second you might do to an old sofa! It's the same word and the same prefix, but just a small line (called a hyphen), that is used to make the different meanings clear.

retro

Meaning: **back, backwards**

retro indicates that something is from the past. It helps us to form some fun compound words and sometimes it appears as a freestanding adjective, as in "retro fashion" or "retro design".

DID YOU KNOW?

We now sometimes use the word "retro" on its own to mean something that is from the past but considered very cool. For example, "Ooh, I love your shoes, they are so retro!"

Other words to learn:

retrograde
deteriorating

retrogress
to deteriorate

retrofitting
adding a part to something that it did not have when manufactured or built

retrospective
looking backwards and considering past events

retrospection
the process of looking backwards and considering past events

retro music
music from the past

retrospect

retro + spect (to look at)
Literal meaning: backwards look

thinking about something in the past

retrofit

retro + fit
Literal meaning: backwards fit

to add something to a machine that it did not have when it was made

retroactive

retro + active
Literal meaning: acting back

having effect from a date in the past

retrorocket

retro + rocket
Literal meaning: backwards rocket

a rocket on a spacecraft that travels in the opposite direction from the spacecraft to try to slow it down

post

Meaning: **after, behind**

post means "after" or "behind" when used as a prefix, but it can also be used as a noun or a verb with many different meanings. It might refer to mail, a job, a fence post, or the place a soldier is told to stand for military duty.

postscript

post + script
Literal meaning: after write

a short message added to a letter after your signature (This is what P.S. stands for!)

postgraduate

post + graduate (step towards)
Literal meaning: an after-step towards something

a student who is studying for a degree after they've already earned a university degree

postpone

post + pone (put)
Literal meaning: to put after

to delay an event or action

PARROT ROCK CONCERT **POSTPONED**

posterity

post + erity (makes a noun)
Literal meaning: coming after

the people who will exist in the future; descendants

Other words to learn:

postbellum
after the American Civil War

postdate
to put a date on a document that is after the date it was created

posterior
at or towards the back

postnatal
after a baby is born

postseason
after a season, often in sports

preposterous
foolish, stupid

DID YOU KNOW?
There are many idioms and fun phrases that have a similar meaning to "preposterous" ("before-behind"), including: topsy-turvy, higgledy-piggledy, hurly-burly, hodgepodge.

CHALLENGE!
You may have heard the phrase "ante meridiem", abbreviated to a.m. and meaning "before midday". What do you think "post meridiem" means, and what is its abbreviation?

After midday; p.m.

ab

Meaning: **from, away, off**

ab is not one of the more common prefixes, but you might find it useful for these kinds of words.

abnormal

ab + normal
Literal meaning: off normal

not usual

absent

ab(s) + ent (to be)
Literal meaning: to be away from

not present

abbreviate

ab + brevi (shorten) + ate (makes a verb)
Literal meaning: to shorten

to make shorter

abseil

ab + seil
Literal meaning: down rope

holding on to a rope that is fixed at the top of a slope, in order to go down

Other words to learn:

abbreviation
a short form of a word or phrase

abduct
to take someone to go somewhere with force

abdicate
to resign from being a king or queen

ablution
washing yourself

absolve
to free or forgive someone, especially in religion or law

abundant
more than enough

CHALLENGE!

Revisit page 92 in this book. Search for one word that begins with the prefix ab, and also appears on this page.

abbreviated/tion

DID YOU KNOW?

You might have expected this word to be spelled as "absail", but it isn't. "Abseil" is quite a new word from the 20th century. It comes from the German word, abseilen, which means to go down (ab) by rope (seilen). There are many examples of English borrowing words from German.

ac/ad

Meaning: **to, towards, near**

ad is sometimes simplified to *a* before words beginning *sc*, *sp* and *st*. It shifts to **ac** before some consonants and can be spelled *af* or *ag* following a consonant. So it can be quite tricky to track!

accelerate

ac + celer (swift) + ate
Literal meaning: to quicken

to make something speed up

accessible

ac + cess (go) + ible (makes an adjective)
Literal meaning: to go to

easy to find or reach

admit

ad + mit (let go)
Literal meaning: to let go

to allow something; to let in

admire

ad + mire (wonder)
Literal meaning: with wonder

to think very highly or favourably of

DID YOU KNOW?

Over the years, the meaning of the word "accessible" has shifted. It used to mean an approach, then it became about being easy to reach, and by the 1960s it was about being able to be easily understood. Nowadays, we use it to talk about things, places, and even ideas that are accessible to all people.

Other words to learn:

accentuate
to emphasise a part of something

accomplish
to finish or achieve something with success

accost
to approach someone in an aggressive way

acquiesce
to agree or accept something begrudgingly

adhere
to stick to something firmly

admiral
the highest rank of naval officer

admiration
thinking very highly of someone or something

adopt
to take responsibility for

CINEMA

CHALLENGE!

Who do you really admire? Why?

circ

Meaning: **around, about**

circ or **circum** comes from the Latin *circus*, which means "circular line" or "ring". The Greek form is very similar: *kirkos*.

circle

circ + le
Literal meaning: little ring

a round flat shape that looks like a ring

circus

circ + us
Literal meaning: ring or circular line

a group of travelling performers who perform in an enclosed tent

circuit

circ + uit
Literal meaning: a going around

a route or sports track that is circular

circumstance

circum + stance (stand)
Literal meaning: surrounding condition

an event or fact that makes a situation how it is

Other words to learn:

circuitous
not a direct or straight path

circulation
the movement of blood around the body

circumnavigate
to sail around something

circumference
the perimeter of a circle

circumspect
cautious about risk taking

circumstances
situation or position

FUN FACT!

The Romans used the word "circus" as the name for circular arenas or theatres for performers and oval courses for games and chariot racing. Nowadays, we might use the word to describe buildings that are arranged in a ring or circle.

CO

Meaning: **together, joint**

co is an easy prefix to remember and use; it's very cooperative!

copilot

co + pilot
Literal meaning: to pilot together

a second pilot

FUN FACT!

In the 1500s, "pilot" referred to someone who steered a ship. By the 1600s, it meant someone who guided the direction of others in a more general sense, and by the 1800s, it included someone who controls a hot-air balloon. Finally, by 1907, it came to mean someone who flies an aeroplane. By 1927, the term "copilot" was in use. The meaning of the word shifted over time to match the developments in transport.

coalition

co + alition (unite)
Literal meaning: unite, grow together

a group formed of different organisations, countries, or people who agree to act together, usually temporarily, to achieve something; similar to an alliance (page 118)

coordinate

co + ordin (order, arrange) + ate
Literal meaning: to arrange together in order

to make several things or people work together

coauthor

co + author
Literal meaning: write together

a writer who writes with another person

Other words to learn:

coexisting
living together in the same place, at the same time

cohesive
working effectively together

cohort
a group of people sharing a similar characteristic, like children in a school year

cooperate
to work together for an agreed purpose; to do what someone asks

correlate
to be connected and affect related things

correlation
a connection between two or more facts

coherent
clear, logical, and easy to understand

incoherent
unclear, not logical, and hard to understand

FUN FACT!

A ghostwriter is a kind of coauthor who writes something for someone else in secret so the public doesn't know. The ghostwriter usually remains anonymous.

em/en

Meaning: **into, cover with, cause**

em and **en** help us form verbs from adjectives and nouns. So the noun "power" becomes the verb "empower" (to make something powerful). The adjective "rich" becomes the verb "enrich" (to make something better or richer).

empower

em + power
Literal meaning: with power

to give someone strength, ability, or confidence to do something

emphasis

em + phasis (show, shine)
Literal meaning: covered with shine

increased importance or attention given to something

enrobe

en + robe
Literal meaning: to clothe

to wrap something in something else

embellish

em + bell (beauty) + ish (makes a verb)
Literal meaning: cover with beauty

to make something more beautiful by adding to it

Other words to learn:

embankment
a bank that stops a river or lake from overflowing

embark
to begin

empathetic
understanding of other people's feelings

empathy
the ability to understand others' feelings as if they were your own

enlarge
to increase in size or expand

envisage
to imagine

emanate
to give out or to emerge from

embody
to be a model example of someone or something

FUN FACT!

Sometimes we use specific words to enrich a description. If we are creating chocolate-dipped strawberries (yum!), the recipe may describe how we enrobe the strawberries in chocolate. This makes it sound like we are clothing the strawberries in chocolate in a luxurious way, which sounds much tastier than "dip them in chocolate".

en/in

Meaning: **in, put in, on, inside, inwards**

Sometimes we find the **en** spelling and sometimes the **in** spelling. People argue about which is correct. Some words can be spelled with either an 'e' or an 'i', so always check the dictionary if you're not sure.

enclose

en + close
Literal meaning: to close in

to surround something with something else

inwards

in + wards
Literal meaning: to turn towards

towards the inside of something

envelope

en + velope (to wrap up)
Literal meaning: to wrap up in

a flat paper container for a letter

infection

in + fect (spoil, stain) + ion (makes a noun)
Literal meaning: fill with disease

bacteria or virus in the body

Other words to learn:

encapsulate/incapsulate
to summarise

endemic
widespread among people

envision
to imagine

include
to add or incorporate

inside
the interior of something

insurance
protection against misfortune

injection
a vaccination

infect
to transmit disease to others

DID YOU KNOW?

Sometimes it helps to chunk a word into its syllables to guide you through its spelling. Look at this word: "encapsulate". It has four syllables: en + cap + su + late. *en* means to put in, but the next two syllables have more meaning if kept together; *capsule* means a small box or chest, and the final syllable *ate* is a verb suffix. So four syllables have three points of meaning.

ex

Meaning: **out**

Not surprisingly, the opposite of **ex** is *in*. So we exhale and inhale, but that doesn't always work since we have "explode" and "implode". Here are some of its many uses!

explain

ex + plain (flat, spread)
Literal meaning: spread out

to give information or describe something to make it clear or easy to understand

exit

ex + it (to go)
Literal meaning: a leaving

way out

extend

ex + tend
Literal meaning: to stretch out

to make something longer or bigger by adding to it

explode

ex + plode (from "plaudere", to clap)
Literal meaning: to clap out

to burst out or cause something to do that

Other words to learn:

excavate
to dig out

exchange
to replace one thing with another

exclaim
to cry or call out

excursion
a short trip

exhale
to breathe out

expertise
special knowledge or skill

explanation
the reason(s) for something

extension
lengthening or addition

CHALLENGE!

If "external" means outside, what does "internal" mean?

inside

DID YOU KNOW?

In the 1500s, "explode" meant to reject something by clapping to drive it out. In the theatre, people might have clapped an actor "off" stage by making a noise, which is strange because we now clap to show that we've enjoyed a performance.

hypo

Meaning: **under, less than normal**

Take great care with **hypo** because its opposite is *hyper*, meaning "over, above, beyond". This is very important to remember when spelling these words, as *hypo* and *hyper* are easy to mix up. Plus, the words tend to be very long!

hypochondriac

hypo + chondr(o) (cartilage) + iac
Literal meaning: person feeling unwell under the cartilage of the breastbone

someone who often thinks they are ill, even when they are well

hypotenuse

hypo + tenuse (stretch)
Literal meaning: under the stretch

the side of a right-angled triangle that is opposite the right angle

hypocrite

hypo + crite (interpreter)
Literal meaning: interpreter from underneath

a person who pretends to have particular morals or opinions, but acts in an opposite way to them

hypothermia

hypo + therm (heat) + ia (abstract noun ending)
Literal meaning: being under heat

a serious illness caused by an abnormally low body temperature

Other words to learn:

hypoglycaemia
when levels of sugar in the blood become too low and may cause unconsciousness

hypocritical
to be false or two-faced

hypocrisy
behaviour that is opposite to what a person claims to think or feel

hypodermic
a needle that goes under the skin

hypothesis
a suggested explanation for something that needs further testing

hypothetical
a circumstance based on assumptions or imagination

FUN FACT!

The Greek word *hypokrites* means "actor". This word comes from actors in ancient Greek theatre who wore large face masks to show which character they were playing, so they acted or interpreted the story from underneath their masks.

LATIN ORIGIN

inter

Meaning: **among, between**

This prefix helps us create powerful compound words such as "international" and "intergalactic". **inter** is all about connections!

internet

inter + net
Literal meaning: between networks

the system of connected computers that allows us to communicate and share information around the world

intergalactic

inter + galactic
Literal meaning: between galaxies

of, existing, or happening between galaxies

interfere

inter + fere (strike, knock)
Literal meaning: between strike

to get involved in a situation that has not got anything to do with you

DID YOU KNOW?

"Betwixt" is an Old English word meaning "between", just like inter. It literally meant "by two-ish" which doesn't tell us much. There is an old expression, "betwixt and between", that describes when someone or something is in a middle position. Maybe they are undecided or just halfway.

intercity

inter + city
Literal meaning: between cities

travelling between one city and another

Other words to learn:

interference
obstruction and meddling

interact
to socialise with others

interlude
an interval or break

intermediate
middle or halfway

interrupt
to disturb or break into

intersection
point at a junction or crossroads

interpretation
explaining something using different words, sometimes in a different language

interview
a meeting, often about work or a new job

FUN FACT!

The Shanghai maglev train is the world's fastest commercial train with a top speed of 431 km (268 miles) per hour. It takes just 8 minutes to travel 30.5 km (19 miles) from the city of Shanghai to its international airport.

intra/intro

Meaning: **within, inside**

Don't confuse **intra** or **intro** with the Greek prefix *inter* on the previous page. It's always worth checking your spelling and thinking about these meanings to see if you've made the correct spelling choice.

FUN FACT!

The words "introvert" and "extrovert" are fairly recent. In 1878 the term "introvert" was used in zoology (the science of studying animals). The sense of it applying to a person was introduced later, in 1917, by a German psychologist, C. G. Jung.

Other words to learn:

intractable
difficult or stubborn

intravenous
connected to or into a vein of the body

introduce
to put something into use for the first time, or to tell someone another person's name the first time they meet

introducer
a person who puts something into use for the first time or who tells another person's name the first time they meet

introject
to adopt the ideas of others without realising it

introspection
examining your own ideas and feelings

introduction

intro + duc (lead) + tion
Literal meaning: to lead inwards

the first part of something

introvert

intro + vert
Literal meaning: someone who turns inwards

someone who enjoys doing things alone or in small groups

intranasal

intra + nasal
Literal meaning: inside the nose

given through the nose, like a vaccine

intranet

intra + net
Literal meaning: inside network

a system of connected computers within an organisation

CHALLENGE!

Are you an introvert or an extrovert? Speak with a friend and explain why you think that.

LATIN ORIGIN

OLD ENGLISH ORIGIN

med/mid

Meaning: **middle**

These two prefixes have different origins. **med** is used in more formal language, like "Medieval". **mid** tends to be used more in everyday English, like "midday".

median

med + ian (makes a noun)
Literal meaning: of the middle

the number that falls directly in the middle of a series of numbers that are ordered from the lowest to the highest

medium

med + ium (makes an adjective)
Literal meaning: the middle

halfway between two extremes

Mediterranean

med + it + terra (land) + nean (makes a noun)
Literal meaning: midland

the lands surrounding the Mediterranean Sea

midnight

mid + night
Literal meaning: middle of the night

the time that is 12 o'clock in the middle of the night

DID YOU KNOW?
We base midnight on the exact moment the sun is over the South Pole, but this can vary slightly over time because of the irregularity of the earth's rotation.

FUN FACT!
The Mediterranean Sea is an extra salty sea because it loses more water to evaporation than it receives from rainfall or rivers. Salt doesn't evaporate, so it gets stronger over time.

Other words to learn:

middling
medium or intermediate

mediator
a person who talks to people to help them find a middle ground

Medieval
related to a period of time in history called the Middle Ages, spanning the late 400s to around the mid-1400s

mediocre
neither very good nor very bad; so-so

midriff
the middle part of the body between the chest and the waist

midway
a halfway point or the middle of something

DID YOU KNOW?

To "strike a happy medium" is to think or act in a way to keep everyone happy because it avoids being extreme!

ob/op

Meaning: **towards, against, before**

Words of Latin origin can be created using **ob** or **op**, but also *oc* and *of*, too. It's an interesting thing to observe.

object

ob + ject
Literal meaning: to set against

to feel or say that you don't approve or agree

obscure

ob + scure (covered)
Literal meaning: over covered

to put something in the way of other things so they can't be seen

oppose

op + pose (to place)
Literal meaning: to place in front of

to disagree with something by speaking or acting against it

observatory

ob + servat (watch) + ory (place for)
Literal meaning: place to watch over

a building from which scientists can watch and study the weather, the stars, the planets, etc.

Other words to learn:

obnoxious
very unpleasant and rude

obstacle
something in the way that blocks movement or progress

observe
to watch

observer
a person who watches

observation
something that has been seen and often recorded or reported

opposite
entirely different, contrasting

opposition
the other team in sport or a disagreement

oppress
to control or keep (people) down by force

FUN FACT!

The Griffith Observatory in Los Angeles, California, is the best place to be able to see the world-famous Hollywood sign. But is also a functional observatory with telescopes for studying the planets and stars.

DID YOU KNOW?

When the word "object" is a verb, we place the stress on the second syllable ("I object to that statement"). When it is a noun, we use it to name a thing ("The object before you is very precious"), and then the stress is on the first syllable.

LATIN ORIGIN

per

Meaning: **completely, through, thorough**

In its sense of "thorough", **per** adds strength of meaning to the root word. It allows perfection!

permeate

per + meate (to pass)
Literal meaning: pass through

to spread through and mix in with something

perfect

per + fect (to make or do)
Literal meaning: completely done

thoroughly done and faultless

permit

per + mit (let go)
Literal meaning: give permission

to allow something to happen

permanent

per + man (remain) + ent (to be)
Literal meaning: remain through

lasting forever or for a long time

Other words to learn:

perennially
continually

permission
consent to do something

persist
to keep doing something

persuade
to talk or coax someone into doing something

persuasive
to be able to coax or convince someone

perform
to carry out an action, sometimes on stage

performer
a person who carries out an action, sometimes onstage

performance
the act of carrying out an action; acting, presenting, singing

CHALLENGE!

"Permit" can also be a noun meaning a licence to do something. The stress is on the first syllable. In the verb, the stress is on the second syllable. Practise saying this sentence with the correct pronunciation: "I permit you to use this permit."

FUN FACT!

Perennials are plants that bloom each year if well cared for. Examples include banana plants, maple trees, mint, chives, and ginger.

105

peri

Meaning: **around, enclosing**

peri is a less common prefix, but nonetheless quite useful. It is not to be confused with *per* as described on the previous page. Know your permissions from your perimeters!

perimeter

peri + meter
Literal meaning: the measure around

a boundary around an area

periphery

peri + phery
Literal meaning: to move around

the edge of an area

period

peri + od (a journey)
Literal meaning: journey around

a length of time

periscope

peri + scope
Literal meaning: an instrument for viewing around

a long vertical tube that gives a view of what is above or around an enclosed space

Other words to learn:

peril
great danger

periodical
a monthly or weekly publication

periodontal
around the tooth

peripatetic
on the move

peripheral
on the edge of an area

perish
to die

FUN FACT!

Peripheral vision is how well you can see near the edges of your viewing. You may have had an eye examination to test this. You have to look straight ahead, rest your head in a chin rest, and look out for spots of light. The spots vary in brightness and colour, and you press a clicker to indicate when you can see the light at the side.

DID YOU KNOW?

In American English, the punctuation marking the end of a sentence is called a period. The original Greek symbol for it used to hover at the top of the line instead of sitting at the bottom, but its meaning of marking the end of a thought has remained the same.

pro

Meaning: **before, in front of, in place of, out**

In fact, **pro** has multiple meanings as you can see from the words below.

LATIN ORIGIN

GREEK ORIGIN

CHALLENGE!

Match the proverb to its correct meaning.

1. Look before you leap!
2. Out of the frying pan into the fire!
3. A stitch in time saves nine!

a. Take swift action to avoid bigger problems later on.
b. Be cautious before taking action.
c. Be careful not to change from a bad situation to one that is worse.

Answers: 1. b; 2. c; 3. a

---

profile

pro + file (draw out a line)
Literal meaning: outline

information about a person's life and interests

pronoun

pro + noun
Literal meaning: in place of the name

a word used in place of a noun to avoid repeating it

pronounce

pro + nounce
Literal meaning: to announce out

to declare something publicly

---

proverb

pro + verb (word)
Literal meaning: words put forwards

a well-known short sentence, stating something commonly experienced or giving advice

---

Other words to learn:

proceed
to begin or go ahead

procession
a parade of people or vehicles moving forwards together

prognosis
a forecast of a likely outcome

prologue
an introduction before the main event or account

protect
to look after and keep safe

programme
a plan for a series of events

provoke
to deliberately annoy or irritate

professional
someone qualified, trained, and skilled for a specific career

---

DID YOU KNOW?

There are lots of different types of pronouns, but you probably first think about personal pronouns, which change according to who is speaking or writing (the first person, I), the person or thing being spoken to (the second person, you) or the person or things being spoken about (the third person, he, she, or it).

LATIN ORIGIN

sec/seg/seque

Meaning: **after, to follow**

You are sure to know some of the words that feature **seque** if you love reading, listening to, or viewing series. One good story is never enough, and we look forward to the sequel.

sequel

seque + l
Literal meaning: that which follows

the continuation of a story

second

sec + ond
Literal meaning: to follow next

next after first

sequence

seque + nce
Literal meaning: a following

a series of things that are linked in a particular order

segue

segue
Literal meaning: to follow

a connection between one piece of music, part of a story, subject, or situation to another

Other words to learn:

consequence
the result of an action

sequential
following an order

sequestered
isolated and withdrawn

prosecute
to bring a legal action against someone who has broken a law

subsequent
following, later

CHALLENGE!

Some of these words to learn include the letters *seque*, but not as a prefix. Look for the letters in each of the words and talk about the word meanings linked to the prefix.

FUN FACT!

When you are on holiday or visiting a city, it's fun to hire a Segway™, which is a two-wheeled electric vehicle that you ride while standing up and have to try to balance on while moving along. It provides a smooth journey (if you drive it well!) and its name was apparently chosen because it is similar to the word "segue".

sub

Meaning: **under, lower than, inferior to**

sub is probably the most common prefix with this meaning, but *suc, suf, sug, sup,* and *sur* all mean "under", too!

submarine

sub + marine (sea, of the sea)
Literal meaning: under the sea

a type of ship that travels above and below the surface of the sea

substitute

sub + stitute (set)
Literal meaning: lower than another

something or someone you can use instead of your first choice

subway

sub + way
Literal meaning: a route under

an underground passage that allows people on foot to cross a busy road (or in the US, an underground railway for electric trains)

subterranean

sub + terra (earth, the ground) + nean (makes an adjective)
Literal meaning: underground

under the ground

Other words to learn:

subject
the thing that is being studied or discussed

submerge
to go or make something go under water

subscribe
to pay for a regular product, often a magazine or podcast

subside
to become weak and dwindle

subsist
to have just enough to live

substandard
inadequate or inferior

subtle
understated or delicate

FUN FACT!

Meerkats live in subterranean burrows that they dig in their desert homes. The burrows have multiple entrances, tunnels, and rooms. The meerkats sleep underground and only emerge in the day.

DID YOU KNOW?

A subheading is a mini heading under the main heading of a piece of writing. It helps to guide a reader to keep reading and to structure their reading.

trans

Meaning: **across, beyond, through**

trans is linked to many words that have to do with travel and transport. In other parts of this book, you may also have come across both *fer* and *port*, which are also linked to this theme and have similar meanings.

translate

trans + late (carried)
Literal meaning: to carry across

to change words into a different language

transparent

trans + parent (appear)
Literal meaning: appear through

easy to see through

transport

trans + port (carry)
Literal meaning: carry across

to carry people or things

transmit

trans + mit (send)
Literal meaning: send across

to pass a disease from one person or animal to another; to broadcast or send out messages via radio, television, etc.

Other words to learn:

transcontinental
crossing a continent

transfer
to move someone or something from one place to another

transform
to change completely, especially to improve

transit
the movement of goods or people from one place to another

translucent
letting some light pass through

transport
the movement of goods or people from one place to another

transmission
the passing on of something from one place to another; the broadcasting of a programme or film

translation
the act of changing words into a different language

FUN FACT!

Some creatures are transparent, which makes it very difficult for their prey to see them. There are examples of transparent butterflies, jellyfish, frogs and snails. While some are only this way while they are young, many stay transparent for their entire lives.

micro

Meaning: **extremely small, short**

micro is linked to many words that are to do with small sizes or amounts. You may have already discovered "microphone" on page 58 and "microscope" on page 63, but now they appear here together with a different focus.

microphone

micro + phone (sound, voice)
Literal meaning: small sound

device that records sounds and can make your voice louder

microchip

micro + chip (small piece)
Literal meaning: very small piece

a very small piece of silicon inside a computer

microscope

micro + scope (observe)
Literal meaning: small viewing

a device that makes very small things look bigger

microbe

micro + be (from bios, "life")
Literal meaning: small life

a very small living thing that can only be seen using a microscope

FUN FACT!

Among all the microbes, *Nanoarchaeum equitans* is generally thought to be the smallest. It was discovered in 2002 on the seafloor just off the coast of Iceland.

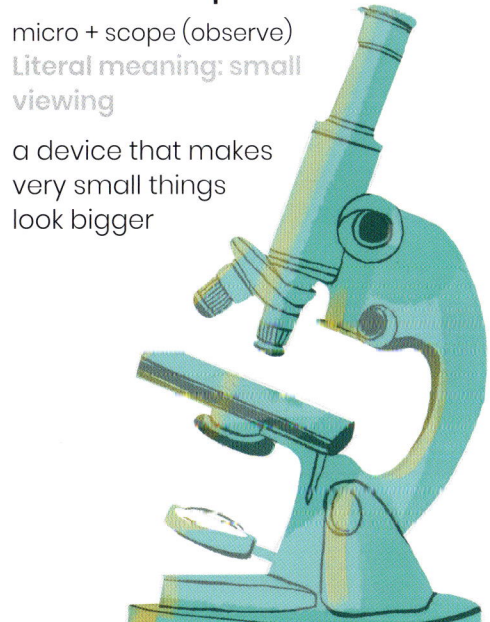

Other words to learn:

microbiologist
a person who studies very small living things

microclimate
a climate that is different from that in the area around it

microfilm
a type of film used for taking a photograph in a reduced size

micromanage
to control every tiny step of something

microprocessor
the main part of a computer that controls how it works

microwave
an electric oven that cooks or heats food fast using waves of energy

DID YOU KNOW?

The earliest microscopes, in use up to about the 1600s, were called flea glasses because they were used to study small insects. Later microscopes had multiple lenses, which meant that even smaller things, like bacteria and cells, could be studied.

LATIN ORIGIN

mini

Meaning: **very small, less**

Just like *micro*, **mini** features in many words that have to do with small sizes or amounts.

minimum

mini + mum
Literal meaning: smallest possible

smallest or least thing

miniature

mini + ature (makes a noun)
Literal meaning: small picture

extremely reduced in size

minute

min + ute
Literal meaning: a small portion or piece (here of time)

a period of time equalling 60 seconds

minimalist

mini + mal + ist (makes a noun)
Literal meaning: minimal artist

someone who likes design, music, or literature to be simple and without decoration

Other words to learn:

minuscule
very small

minim
a note in music that equals two quarter notes (crotchets)

minions
unimportant followers of a powerful person

minimal
the least or smallest amount

minutiae
the tiniest of details

miniseries
a TV show divided into short parts and shown over a short time

DID YOU KNOW?

"Minute" as an adjective requires a different pronunciation with the emphasis on the second syllable and means exceptionally tiny.

FUN FACT!

An artist who paints small pictures is called a miniaturist. Jean Petitot (1607—1691) was a French-Swiss enamel painter and is said to be one of the greatest miniaturists in the history of art. Some of his portraits measure just 3.1 cm (1.25 inches) across.

CHALLENGE!

What is the opposite of minimum?

maximum

omni

Meaning: **all**

omni really is a very grand kind of prefix because it always implies big general ideas.

omnipotent

omni + potent (powerful)
Literal meaning: all powerful

having unlimited power

omniscient

omni + scient (knowledge)
Literal meaning: all knowledge

knowing all things

omnipresent

omni + present (be before)
Literal meaning: present everywhere

present in all places at all times

CHALLENGE!

If carnivores eat meat and herbivores eat plants, what do you think omnivores eat?

Everything, because omni means "all"!

omnibus

omni + bus
Literal meaning: bus for all

an old-fashioned bus

Other words to learn:

omnichannel
a way to buy things from the same business whether from a computer, an app, or in a shop

omnific
creating all things

omnipotence
the state of having unlimited power

omniscience
the state of knowing all things

omnivorous
eating both plants and meat

FUN FACT!

Buses were invented in France in 1662. They started off as horse-drawn carriages that ran to a timed schedule across the streets of Paris. It was many years later when a kind of steam-engine bus was driven, and nowadays many buses have moved from petrol and diesel models to electric.

super

Meaning: **beyond highest**

super is all about the best of the best. You'll be thinking about superheroes, the Super Bowl in the US, and all things superb and super-duper!

FUN FACT!

A single supernova releases as much energy as our sun will in its predicted entire 10-billion-year life span. One supernova can, for a short time, outshine billions of stars in an entire galaxy!

Other words to learn:

superfluous
more than is needed

superimpose
to overlay or cover something with something else

superior
better in some way, first-rate

superlative
the best compared to others

supermarket
a large shop that sells groceries

supervisor
a person who manages others, usually at work

superstructure
the part of a building that is above the ground

supreme
the best or very great

superhero

super + hero
Literal meaning: the best protector

a character in a comic, cartoon, or film who fights for good against evil using special powers

superficial

super + ficial (face, surface)
Literal meaning: above the surface

not important or meaningful

supernova

super + nova (new)
Literal meaning: beyond new

a powerful, bright explosion of a star

supersonic

super + sonic (sound)
Literal meaning: sound waves beyond normal hearing

faster than the speed of sound

CHALLENGE!

How many superheroes can you name? Who is your personal superhero?

ultra

Meaning: **beyond, extreme, more than**

ultra, like *super*, is all about the best of the best. But this time, you'll be thinking how ultracool you are for knowing so many prefixes!

ultrasound

ultra + sound
Literal meaning: extreme sound

a machine that uses sound waves, especially for medical checks

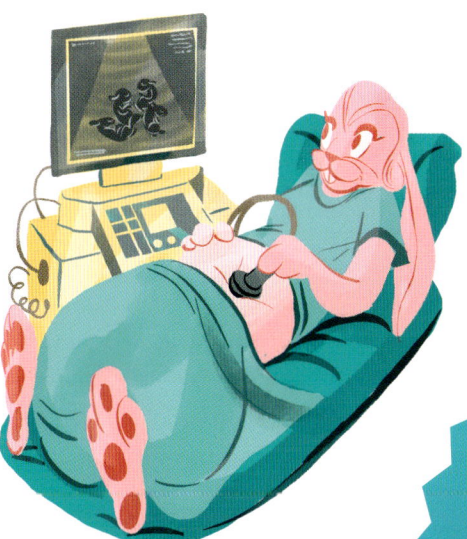

ultramarathon

ultra + marathon
Literal meaning: extremely long-distance footrace

a running race that is longer than a marathon (a race that is about 42 km or 26 miles)

ultramodern

ultra + modern
Literal meaning: extreme modernity

very new and up-to-date

ultrahigh

ultra + high
Literal meaning: extreme height

at a very great height

Other words to learn:

ultracautious
very risk averse, careful

ultraclean
very hygienic

ultracool
very good or fashionable

ultraheavy
very weighty

ultralight
very airy

ultrasonic
having a sound that is too high for people to hear

ultramarine
a bright blue colour

DID YOU KNOW?

The highest mountain in the world, on land, is Mount Everest, which stands at 8,850 m (29,035 ft). But there is an ultrahigh mountain called Mauna Kea in Hawai'i that starts at the bottom of the ocean and reaches up to snow-covered mountain peaks. It stands at 10,210 m (33,500 ft). Now that is ultrahigh!

FUN FACT!

Imagine it's 490 BCE in ancient Greece. The Greeks are fighting the Persians, and after a long battle, the Greeks win. The Greeks need to communicate their victory to those in the main Greek city of Athens, so they send a messenger called Pheidippides. Legend tells us that he ran all the way from Marathon to Athens to deliver the good news!

Suffixes

Noun suffixes

Verb suffixes

Adjective suffixes

Adverb suffixes

NOUN SUFFIXES

If a word uses a suffix to turn itself into a noun, it's an abstract noun rather than a concrete noun. Concrete nouns are physical things that can be seen, touched, heard, tasted, or smelled. Abstract nouns are not physical and cannot be sensed.

LATIN ORIGIN

age

Meaning: **belonging to, process**

The suffix **age** can be used to change a word, usually a verb, into a noun. Take courage! "Courage" is an abstract noun.

break**age**

break + age
Literal meaning: the act of breaking

the act of breaking something or something that has been broken

FUN FACT!

In 600 BCE, Romans started building aqueducts to bring fresh water into a city and take away all of the sewage (poo and pee). Before that, some people would just throw their waste out of their window and onto the street!

pack**age**

pack + age
Literal meaning: the process of packing

a bundle or parcel

sew**age**

sew (drain) + age
Literal meaning: the process of draining water

waste such as water, pee, or poo

bever**age**

bever (drink) + age
Literal meaning: the process of drinking

a drink

Other words to learn:

appendage
anything that is joined to something larger

coverage
how much something is reported, especially in the news

storage
a space where something is kept; the capacity of space for keeping things, including on a computer

courage
bravery

damage
harm done to someone or something

image
a picture or idea of someone or something

ance

Meaning: **state, quality**

ance is used to create nouns, and it operates very similarly to *ence* (page 120). In spelling, you have to really watch out for using the correct suffix so that you don't muddle them!

brilli**ance**

brilli (sparkle, shine) + ance
Literal meaning: the quality of sparkling

excellence or distinction in something

perform**ance**

perform (completely provide) + ance
Literal meaning: the state of completing something

entertaining an audience by doing something such as singing, dancing, or acting

annoy**ance**

annoy + ance
Literal meaning: the state of being annoyed

the feeling of being annoyed, when someone makes you angry or impatient

alli**ance**

alli (bind to, tie to) + ance
Literal meaning: the quality of being bound or tied together

a group of countries, political parties, or people who have agreed to work together because of shared interests or aims; similar to "coalition" (page 98)

Other words to learn:

acceptance
agreeing or saying yes to a proposal or invitation

relevance
the significance or importance of something to a situation or person

disturbance
disorder or upset

finance
the business of managing money

reliance
depending on something or someone

surveillance
constant observation of a place or person

CHALLENGE!
How do you shine? What is your brilliance?

OLD ENGLISH ORIGIN

dom

Meaning: **condition, state, or realm**

dom is another suffix that creates a noun, whether from a verb or another noun. Find your freedom! "Freedom" is an abstract noun.

boredom

bore + dom
Literal meaning: the state of being bored

the state of being bored

king**dom**

king + dom
Literal meaning: the realm of a king

a place under the control of a person (a king or queen), or a group of things (the plant kingdom, the animal kingdom)

FUN FACT!

"Are you as bored as I am?" Read that question backwards to see how it still makes sense. That should help you to avoid boredom!

wis**dom**

wis (know) + dom
Literal meaning: the realm of knowledge

the ability to use what you've learned through experience to make good decisions

star**dom**

star + dom
Literal meaning: the realm of stars

the state of being very famous, as a celebrity

Other words to learn:

chiefdom
the region ruled by a chief

fandom
the state of being a fan of someone or something; the name for a group of fans

freedom
the right to do, say, think whatever you want without control or limit

officialdom
a group of people in a position of power who stop you from doing what you want to do because of the rules

ence

Meaning: **condition, state**

You may have already read about another suffix, *ance*, that along with **ence** often causes spelling problems for us. Go back to page 118 to read more about it. Have confidence! "Confidence" is an abstract noun.

audi**ence**

audi (hear) + ence
Literal meaning: the state of hearing

a group of people watching or listening to a play, concert, film, or public meeting

differ**ence**

dif (apart) + fer (carry, set) + ence
Literal meaning: to set apart

the way two or more things are not the same

resili**ence**

re (back) + sili (jump) + ence
Literal meaning: jump back

the quality of being strong and brave when facing challenges; able to recover from bad situations

intellig**ence**

inte (between) llig (collect) + ence
Literal meaning: collect between

the ability to learn and understand

Other words to learn:

confidence
trust or belief in yourself or others

consequence
an outcome of something

evidence
proof that something is true

existence
the fact of something being real in the world

patience
calmness and tolerance; willingness to wait

reference
a comment about a particular thing or person, or a word, phrase, or idea from another source that is used to make a point about something

CHALLENGE!

What do you understand by the phrase, "audience participation"?

when people watching an event join in or take part in some way

DID YOU KNOW?

When people say this phrase: "You have to face the consequences", they mean that you have to face up to what you have created. So, if you eat too much chocolate and then you feel sick, you are facing the consequences. Oops!

LATIN ORIGIN

er

Meaning: **a person who does an action**

We add this suffix to create a noun representing a person or other living thing. It mainly tells us what they do for a profession or as a hobby. **er** creates concrete nouns because they are words that represent living things.

teach**er**

teach + er
Literal meaning: guide or instructor

someone who teaches

barb**er**

barb (beard) + er
Literal meaning: beard shaver and hair cutter

someone who cuts hair

bak**er**

bak (roast) + er
Literal meaning: someone who roasts food

someone who bakes things like bread and cakes

driv**er**

driv + er
Literal meaning: herdsman, driver of livestock

someone who drives a vehicle

Other words to learn:

astrologer
someone who studies the movements of the stars and uses the information to tell people about how their lives will be

banker
someone who works in banking

builder
someone who constructs, maintains, and renovates buildings

composer
someone who writes music

farmer
someone who owns, manages, or works on the land to tend animals or grow crops

gardener
someone who grows and takes care of plants in a garden

lawyer
someone who gives people advice about the law and represents them in a court of law

painter
someone who paints pictures, or someone who paints buildings

FUN FACT!

When Henry VIII was King of England, barbers cut hair, let blood (they believed that if you were unwell, releasing blood a little might help you feel better), and took care of your teeth, too. Even today, old-fashioned barbers display a red-and-white pole (the barber's pole), outside their shop as this was supposed to represent the binding of the arm of people who had been in to have their blood lot!

eer

Meaning: **a person who does an action**

We add this suffix to create a noun about people in a similar way to *er*. It tells us about someone who does something. **eer** creates concrete nouns because these are words that relate to people.

puppet**eer**

puppet + eer
Literal meaning: puppet player

someone who operates puppets in a theatre

mountain**eer**

mountain + eer
Literal meaning: mountain climber

someone who climbs mountains

volunt**eer**

volunt + eer
Literal meaning: one who acts of their own free will

someone who does something for free, usually to help others

pion**eer**

pion (pawn) + eer
Literal meaning: person who goes first

someone who is one of the first people to do something

Other words to learn:

auctioneer
a person in charge of the selling and buying of things at an auction

sightseer
someone who travels to visit interesting places as a tourist

engineer
a person who designs, constructs, and maintains engines and machines or structures such as bridges

pamphleteer
a writer or publisher of pamphlets

racketeer
a person who makes money from illegal behaviour and actions

DID YOU KNOW?
"Mountaineer" originally meant someone who lived in the mountains, but in the 1800s it changed to mean a mountain climber.

DID YOU KNOW?
Be careful because eer has other meanings, too. "Career" is not someone who cares, and a "reindeer" is not someone who rains or reigns! Remember to always check the meaning when trying to work out what a suffix can do for you.

OLD ENGLISH ORIGIN

hood

Meaning: **state, condition, position**

We add **hood** to create abstract nouns about the appearance or condition of something.

adult**hood**

adult (grown up) + hood
Literal meaning: the state of being grown up

the time of life when you are an adult (usually over the age of 18 or 21)

knight**hood**

knight + hood
Literal meaning: state of being in the military of a king or queen

in the United Kingdom and some other countries, the rank of knight is a special award for special achievements

child**hood**

child (infant, newly born) + hood
Literal meaning: the state of being an infant

the time of life when you are a child

likeli**hood**

likeli (probable) + hood
Literal meaning: state of being probable

the chance that something will happen

Other words to learn:

brotherhood
affection and loyalty for people with whom you have something in common

falsehood
an untrue statement

livelihood
a means of subsistence or income

motherhood
the state of being a mother

neighbourhood
an area where people live

sisterhood
affection and loyalty that women feel for other women with whom they have someone in common

CHALLENGE!

What do you think is the likelihood of the sports team you support winning something this year?

FUN FACT!

Early childhood is thought to be from birth to age 5, middle childhood from ages 6 to 12 and adolescence from ages 13 to 18. What stage of childhood are you in?

ist

Meaning: **a person who does an action**

We add **ist** to create nouns about people doing an action. It is similar to suffixes *er* (page 121) and *eer* (page 122). **ist** creates concrete nouns because these are words that relate to people.

art**ist**

art + ist
Literal meaning: one who does art

someone who paints, makes sculptures, or draws

pian**ist**

pian + ist
Literal meaning: one who plays the piano

someone who plays the piano

flor**ist**

flor (flower) + ist
Literal meaning: one who cares for flowers

someone who prepares and sells or grows flowers and plants

dent**ist**

dent (tooth) + ist
Literal meaning: one who cares for teeth

someone who is qualified to examine and treat people's teeth

DID YOU KNOW?

The suffix *ister* can be used in the same way as *ist*. A "chorister" is one who sings, and a "barrister" is one who stands at the bar in a court of law. This is different from a "barista", who makes coffee in a coffee shop!

Other words to learn:

arborist
someone who plants and tends to trees

pharmacist
someone who is qualified to prepare and sell medicines in a pharmacy

activist
someone who campaigns for social or political change

linguist
someone who is good at learning and using different languages

specialist
someone who has a special skill or knowledge about something in particular

violinist
someone who plays the violin

LATIN ORIGIN

ism

Meaning: **state, quality**

We add **ism** to create abstract nouns, too, but to tell us about states or qualities rather than actions.

Other words to learn:

altruism
a sense of selflessness or being concerned for others over your own needs

dynamism
a sense of energy and drive

idealism
a belief in or the drive for near-perfection

optimism
a sense of positivity

pessimism
a sense of negativity

pacifism
a belief in or the drive for peaceful solutions to challenges and conflicts

tour**ism**

tour (a circuit or excursion) + ism
Literal meaning: an excursion

the business of providing holidays for people

journal**ism**

journal (daily) + ism
Literal meaning: a day's work

the business of writing news articles for print or online news channels

organ**ism**

organ (form) + ism
Literal meaning: a living form

a living plant, animal, bacteria, etc.

hero**ism**

hero + ism
Literal meaning: the quality of a demi-god (nearly being a god)

the quality of being brave and doing great things to help others

DID YOU KNOW?

If you are an optimist, you are full of optimism and see the best of everything. If you are a pessimist, you are full of pessimism and see the worst of everything. Don't know which you are? Look at the picture and ask yourself "Is the glass half empty or half full?"

ity

Meaning: **state, condition, quality**

We add **ity** to create abstract nouns from adjectives.
I hope this is clear enough. I am trying to offer you clarity.

FUN FACT!

Do you know this old rhyme?
Jack be nimble,
Jack be quick,
Jack jump over the candlestick!
What does it mean? There are two thoughts about its meaning. One is that long ago it was considered good luck to jump over a lit candle without putting it out. The other is more fun. There was an old English pirate called "Black Jack Smatt", whose agility was famous, especially when it came to escaping capture.

agility

agil + ity
Literal meaning: the state of being nimble or quick

the condition of being able to move quickly and easily

equality

equal (level) + ity
Literal meaning: state of being equal

fair treatment among different groups of people

clarity

clar (clear) + ity
Literal meaning: state of being clear or bright

a state of being clear and easy to understand, see, or hear

cruelty

cruel (unfeeling, hard-hearted) + ty
Literal meaning: state of being unfeeling, hard-hearted

deliberately unkind behaviour

Other words to learn:

charity
an organisation that raises money to help those in need

civility
formal politeness

ability
the power or quality to do something

necessity
the fact of something being essential and unavoidable

normality
a state of all being in order and routine

reality
real things, facts, truth

LATIN ORIGIN

ment

Meaning: **the action of doing or feeling something**

We add **ment** to create nouns from verbs. I hope you are enjoying this book. Your enjoyment is important to me! "Enjoyment" is an abstract noun.

disappoint**ment**

dis + appoint + ment
Literal meaning: the opposite of fulfilling something

unhappiness when things don't work out the way you wanted them to

refresh**ment**

re + fresh + ment
Literal meaning: to repeat freshening up

the act or sense of being renewed – nowadays often meaning by providing drinks and food

govern**ment**

govern (rule) + ment
Literal meaning: act of ruling

a group of people who officially control a country

achieve**ment**

achieve + ment
Literal meaning: act of completing

the action of working hard to do something good

Other words to learn:

enjoyment
a pleasant feeling from doing something that you like

embarrassment
a feeling of shame or distress

movement
changing position or moving from one place to another

placement
positioning something or someone in a particular place

punishment
correcting or disciplining someone in a particular way

shipment
the sending of a particular kind of cargo by any means of transport to another country

DID YOU KNOW?

"Disappointment" is a word people often misspell. They forget the double 'p' (disapoint) and sometimes add double 's' (dissappoint) instead! It might help you if you remember that there is a spelling 'app' in "disappointment". And this works for related words like "disappear" and "disapprove", too.

ness

Meaning: **action, state, quality**

Yes, **ness** is another suffix we add to adjectives to create nouns. It sounds ridiculous, but ridiculousness is not what we are aiming for here.

dark**ness**

dark (without light) + ness
Literal meaning: the quality of no light

a state of little or no light

kind**ness**

kind (like family) + ness
Literal meaning: the quality of being like family

a quality of being caring or helpful

shy**ness**

shy (timid, easily frightened) + ness
Literal meaning: the quality of being timid

a quality of being nervous and uncomfortable with others

wit**ness**

wit (see) + ness
Literal meaning: the quality of seeing something

someone who sees an event as it happens, especially an accident or crime

Other words to learn:

awkwardness
the quality of being difficult to deal with, use, or do

bossiness
the quality of telling others what to do

happiness
the state of being pleased and content

illness
the state of being unwell with a disease or sickness

ridiculousness
the quality of being silly or stupid

sadness
the state of being unhappy

CHALLENGE!

Do you know what it means when you say that someone is a "dark horse"? Is it:
a. They look and move like a horse.
b. They are not what they first seem; they are surprising.
c. They like horse riding.

q

LATIN ORIGIN

or

Meaning: **a person who does something**

or is a bit like *ist* (page 124), *eer* (page 122), and *er* (page 121) because it's all about what people do. *or* creates concrete nouns because these are words that relate to people.

translat**or**

trans (over) + lat (carried) + or
Literal meaning: one who carries over

someone who changes words from one language into another

invent**or**

invent + or
Literal meaning: one who discovers

someone who designs and creates new things from new ideas

auth**or**

auth + or
Literal meaning: one who makes or creates

someone who writes as a profession

surviv**or**

sur (over) + viv (live) + or
Literal meaning: one who outlives someone else

a person who continues to live, despite having faced very dangerous or deadly circumstances

Other words to learn:

actor
a person who performs in a play, on TV, or in films

advisor (sometimes this is spelled –er)
a person who offers advice and guidance

director
a person who controls, directs, and regulates

governor
the elected head of any US state; a person who directs an organisation or institution

legislator
a person involved in lawmaking

predictor
someone or something that helps you to guess what will happen

FUN FACT!

Matthew Sleman from New Jersey, in the US, became an inventor at just 7 years old. What did he invent? Colour-changing building blocks! They are plastic aquabricks, and they are white when dry. However, when they are wet, the white paint becomes clear and reveals a new colour.

ship

Meaning: **state, condition, skill**

ship is a bit like *ance*, *dom*, *ence*, *hood*, *ism*, *ity*, and *ness*. They all create nouns from adjectives, and for some, from verbs. These are words that cannot be sensed (using our five senses) so we call them abstract rather than concrete.

author**ship**

auth + or + ship
Literal meaning: the formal connection between the author and the work

the state of being the person who wrote something particular

citizen**ship**

citizen (city-dweller) + ship
Literal meaning: the state of living in a city

the state of belonging to a particular country

relation**ship**

relation (connection) + ship
Literal meaning: the state of being connected

the way in which two things are connected

friend**ship**

friend + ship
Literal meaning: the state of having friends

the state of being friends with someone

CHALLENGE!

Name a few friends who are in your friendship group. Do you have a friendship group name or a symbol such as friendship bracelets?

Other words to learn:

apprenticeship
a training period to learn new skill

headship
the condition of being a chief or leader

membership
the condition of belonging to a group; being a member

ownership
the condition of owning something

partnership
the condition of working with two or more people to share risks and rewards

township
a subdivision of a county in certain countries

OLD ENGLISH ORIGIN

th

Meaning: **state, quality**

th creates nouns from adjectives, but these words create meanings that cannot be sensed (using our five senses), so they are abstract rather than concrete.

warm**th**

warm + th
Literal meaning: quality of being warm

a high temperature that is comfortable but not too hot

streng**th**

streng (strong) + th
Literal meaning: quality of physical power

how strong something or someone is

dep**th**

dep (deep) + th
Literal meaning: quality of extension downwards

how deep something is from the top to the bottom

leng**th**

leng (long) + th
Literal meaning: quality of extending along

how long something is

Other words to learn:

breadth
the space between the two sides of something; width

growth
the increase of something

health
the condition of something or someone

stealth
secrecy or slyness

truth
the facts about something

birth
human or animal delivery into the world

CHALLENGE!
What is the length of a football pitch? If you don't know, how can you find out?

2M DEEP

FUN FACT!
If you want to remain strong or improve your strength, you need to think about the muscles in your body. Most people have more than 600! Muscles help to pump blood throughout your body, to move, and to lift heavy objects. Even your heart is a muscle. You can exercise other muscles to improve your strength.

sion

Meaning: **state, quality**

sion creates abstract nouns from verbs. Look at this spelling table to understand some of the rules about how adding the suffix *sion* can affect spellings.

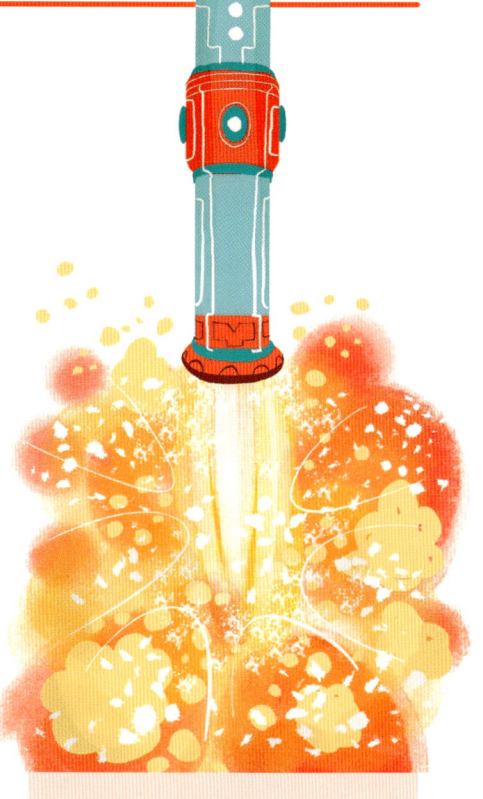

Description	What you do	Like this
Root word ending in **ss**	Remove one **s** and add **sion**	possess
		posses
		possession
Root word ending in **de**	Remove **de** and add **sion**	decide
		deci
		decision
Root word ending in **se**	Remove **se** and add **sion**	tense
		ten
		tension
Root word ending in **mit**	Remove **t** and add **ssion**	admit
		admi
		admission
Root word ending in **d**	Remove **d** and add **sion**	comprehend
		comprehen
		comprehension

ten**sion**

ten (stretch) + sion
Literal meaning: being in state of stretch

feeling tight or stressed, or when something is stretched to the limit

posses**sion**

posses (hold in one's control) + sion
Literal meaning: the state of owning or control

ownership

explo**sion**

ex (out) + plo (cap) + sion
Literal meaning: driving out with violence and noise

an act of bursting out

comprehen**sion**

com (together) + prehen (take) + sion
Literal meaning: take into the mind

complete understanding

Other words to learn:

admission
permission to enter somewhere

confusion
disorder or lack of clarity

conclusion
the findings or result at the end of something

discussion
people talking together about something

excursion
a short journey, trip, or visit

persuasion
the act of urging or influencing someone

LATIN ORIGIN

tion

Meaning: **state, quality, action**

Just like *sion*, **tion** creates abstract nouns from verbs. How is your attention span? Proceed with caution to avoid frustration.

atten**tion**

at (to) + ten (stretch) + tion
Literal meaning: to give heed to (to stretch towards)

focus on something

correc**tion**

correc (straight) + tion
Literal meaning: to put straight

making something right

loca**tion**

loca (place) + tion
Literal meaning: the place of settling

where something is situated

celebra**tion**

celebra (assemble to honour) + tion
Literal meaning: act of assembling to honour

a party to acknowledge something special

Other words to learn:

caution
carefulness

concentration
focus, attention

definition
the meaning of a word; clarity

frustration
a feeling when something you want is prevented

invention
the act of creating something for the first time

population
all the people who live in a country

FUN FACT!

La Tomatina is a food fight celebration held on the last Wednesday of August each year in the town of Buño near Valencia, Spain. Don't worry, the people aren't wasting food – the tomatoes are overripe so can't be eaten!

DID YOU KNOW?

Attention spans are related to age. So 4-year-olds might concentrate for 8–12 minutes, 8-year-olds for 16–24 minutes and 16-year-olds for 32–48 minutes. Some people think using fidget spinners can help engage parts of the brain essential for paying attention.

133

ate

Meaning: **cause to become**

ate is a suffix for Latin verbs. The verb is made by adding the suffix.

VERB SUFFIXES

If a word uses a suffix to turn itself into a verb, it's called a verb suffix. There are few that can really help you deepen your understanding of vocabulary, activate new understandings, and organise your thoughts. On the other hand, there are some exceptions that might complicate things! This section is all about verb suffixes.

complicate

com (together) + plic (fold, weave) + ate
Literal meaning: fold together

to make something difficult to do or understand

terminate

termin (end) + ate
Literal meaning: cause to end

to end something

activate

activ + ate
Literal meaning: cause to become active

to make something move or work

germinate

germin (to sprout) + ate
Literal meaning: cause to sprout

to sprout from a spore, bud, or seed

Other words to learn:

navigate
to steer or direct

cooperate
to work together, collaborate

dedicate
to commit or devote, usually time

dominate
to overshadow or control

evaporate
to disappear, dry up, or fade away

medicate
to give medical treatment

DID YOU KNOW!

In some cases there is no difference between the adjective and the verb forms of a word. We can see that in words such as "dry" (I am dry; I dry my hands); "empty" (My bins are empty; I empty my bins on Mondays); and "warm" (I am warm; I warm my hands). You have to be alert to these no-change words.

LATIN ORIGIN

en

Meaning: **cause to be**

en is used to make verbs. So the adjective "bright" changes to "brighten" and the noun "length" changes to "lengthen" with no complicated changes.

worsen

wors (e) + en
Literal meaning: cause to be mixed up

to make something worse

frighten

fright (fear) + en
Literal meaning: strike with fear

to scare someone

shorten

short + en
Literal meaning: cause to be less

to make something shorter

straighten

straight + en
Literal meaning: cause to be straight

to make something not bent or curved

Other words to learn:

blacken
to make darker

brighten
to make lighter

thicken
to make thicker or more complicated

tighten
to make closer-fitting

toughen
to make harder

flatten
to make smoother

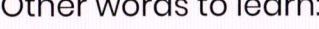

FUN FACT!

Cardboard boxes can be recycled several times and used to make new packaging boxes and sometimes furniture, too. Just empty, dry, clean, and flatten boxes before taking them to the recycling centre.

CHALLENGE!

If Benjamin shortens his name to Ben, and Francesca shortens her name to Fran, what does Jonathon shorten his name to?

Jon

able/ible

Meaning: **can be, able to be, or capable of**

able and **ible** are suffixes that change verbs into adjectives. As a general rule, if you remove *able* from a word, you are left with a complete word. If you remove *ible* from a word, you are left with an incomplete word.

ADJECTIVE SUFFIXES

Did you know? If a word uses a suffix to turn itself into an adjective, it's called an adjective suffix. I know you are more than capable, so you may think this name was entirely predictable. There are some occasional tricky rules to navigate, but you will be thankful that the essential rules are quite sensible.

invis**ible**

in + vis + ible
Literal meaning: incapable of being seen

not able to be seen

unread**able**

un + read + able
Literal meaning: not able to be read

not readable or legible

flex**ible**

flex + ible
Literal meaning: capable of flexing or bending

easy to bend or be bent without breaking

inflat**able**

inflat (blow into) + able
Literal meaning: able to blow air in

able to be filled with air

Other words to learn:

adorable
lovable, attractive

audible
able to be heard

believable
possibly or probably true

divisible
can be divided into smaller parts

predictable
can be anticipated, is likely

responsible
at fault; in charge of something or someone

sensible
having or showing good judgment or sense

unmissable
impossible to miss; must be seen

FUN FACT!

The world's largest inflatable bouncy castle is a tourist attraction in Karachi, Pakistan. It's large enough for 200 people to bounce at once!

al

Meaning: **related to, like**

al is a suffix that creates adjectives from nouns.

central

centr (e) + al
Literal meaning: related to the centre of something

to do with the centre of a place or object

natural

natur (e) + al
Literal meaning: like nature

to do with nature and not involving anything made or done by people

criminal

crimin + al
Literal meaning: related to crime

someone who commits a crime

seasonal

season + al
Literal meaning: related to seasons

to do with particular times of the year according to the seasons

Other words to learn:

accidental
unexpected or unplanned

critical
essential, of utmost importance

musical
tuneful, having talent in music

occasional
rare or infrequent

personal
belonging to self or a particular person

FUN FACT!

Tropical seasonal forests are also known as monsoon forests, and they grow in regions of the world that have a tropical climate, including the Atlantic forests of Brazil and the Guinean seasonal forests of West Africa. Countries like Cambodia, Vietnam, Thailand, and Australia also have seasonal forests.

DID YOU KNOW?

al can also be added to nouns with the meaning "the action of". So, the noun "approval" has the meaning "the act of approving something".

ful

Meaning: **full of**

ful changes a verb into an adjective. Be careful not to add *full* instead of *ful*, but remember that "full" is a word in its own right. Is your brain full of facts about where words come from?

beauti**ful**

beaut (pretty) + i + ful
Literal meaning: full of prettiness

very attractive

wonder**ful**

wonder (object of astonishment) + ful
Literal meaning: full of astonishment

extremely good

mouth**ful**

mouth + ful
Literal meaning: full mouth

an amount of food that fills the mouth

tear**ful**

tear + ful
Literal meaning: full of tears

close to tears or crying

Other words to learn:

delightful
pleasant or entertaining

forgetful
not able to remember easily

hopeful
full of optimism

thankful
full of thanks

wistful
full of longing for something you had

careful
full of care

FUN FACT!

You may or may not know of a song called, "What a Wonderful World" sung by Louis Armstrong in 1967, Louis loved the song because it made him think about his own life, family and home, and how beautiful the world is. But he famously said, "it ain't the world that's so bad, but what we're doing to it. And all I'm saying is, see, what a wonderful world it would be if only we'd give it a chance".

DID YOU KNOW?

If the root word ends in a 'y', change it to an 'i'. So, "beauty" becomes "beautiful", and "plenty" becomes "plentiful".

ial

Meaning: **relates to, of, like**

ial changes the root word into an adjective.

init**ial**

init + ial
Literal meaning: a beginning

relating to being first or the beginning

financ**ial**

financ (payment) + ial
Literal meaning: relating to payment

relating to money and how it is managed

fac**ial**

fac (e) + ial
Literal meaning: of the face

relating to the face

resident**ial**

resident + ial
Literal meaning: serving as a home

relating to living or sleeping somewhere

DID YOU KNOW?

The suffix ial usually appears as cial after a vowel, as in "crucial", and as tial after a consonant, as in "essential". But there are always exceptions to rules, as in "initial" and "financial"!

Other words to learn:

confidential
secret, private

crucial
extremely important or necessary

essential
needed or necessary

potential
an ability to develop or succeed

social
comfortable in the company of others

special
not usual

OLD ENGLISH ORIGIN

y

Meaning: **full of, characterised by**

y used as a suffix can change words into adjectives.

cloud**y**

cloud + y
Literal meaning: full of cloud

dull or overcast

spook**y**

spook + y
Literal meaning: full of fear

frightening or eerie

furr**y**

fur + r + y
Literal meaning: full of cover

like or covered with hair, fur, or fleece

smok**y**

smok(e) + y
Literal meaning: full of smoke

full of smoke or having a grey colour

Other words to learn:

creaky
squeaky or grating

funny
amusing or silly

greasy
fatty or slippery

jumpy
uneasy or nervous

lengthy
very long, overlong

shiny
bright or gleaming

sixty
the number 60

CHALLENGE!

Look at the nouns "fun" and "shake". Add the y and say what you have to do to make the correct spelling.

fun + n + y = funny, double the n; shak(e) + y = shaky, drop the e before adding the y

DID YOU KNOW?

The suffix y can also be a noun suffix in real names like Poppy and Freddy; or in nouns with the meaning of "condition or quality" like "history" and "victory".

OLD ENGLISH ORIGIN

ish

Meaning: **having the nature or character of**

ish changes nouns into adjectives. It also makes the meaning of words a bit vague. It's like saying, "it's there or thereabouts".

fool**ish**

fool + ish
Literal meaning: in the nature of a fool

prone to making mistakes or unwise choices

styl**ish**

styl (e) + ish
Literal meaning: fond of fashion

fashionable and attractive

book**ish**

book + ish
fond of books

loving books or studying

self**ish**

self + ish
Literal meaning: fond of self

only thinking about yourself and not thinking about other people's feelings or needs

Other words to learn:

babyish
like a baby

blondish
blonde in colour

feverish
like a fever

nightmarish
like a nightmare

DID YOU KNOW?

We can also add *ish* to adverbs and prepositions, too: The park is nearish to the station, meaning that the park is somewhat near the station. We can add *ish* to talk about numbers, times, and quantities, too: The birthday party starts at fourish.

FUN FACT!

From around 1892 the term "fool's gold" was used to describe iron pyrite, which is a mineral found in rocks. It looks like gold but is not valuable. You might feel foolish if you think you've discovered gold when it's just iron pyrite!

ive

Meaning: **tending to, doing**

ive changes words into adjectives.

competit**ive**

com (together) + petit (to strive) + ive
Literal meaning: strive after something with others

wanting to win very much

FUN FACT!
Some people say the most expensive thing in the world is the International Space Station. Valuations and the value of money shift over time, but it is thought to be worth in the region of $150 billion.

act**ive**

act + ive
Literal meaning: tending to movement

moving often and regularly

pass**ive**

pass + ive
Literal meaning: tending to suffer

allowing other people to take action and control

expens**ive**

expens(e) + ive
Literal meaning: tending to be costly

costing a lot of money

Other words to learn:

alternative
a substitute or choice

cohesive
united and working together well

cooperative
social, shared

creative
imaginative, inspired

investigative
researching or fact-finding

productive
effective, dynamic, plentiful

DID YOU KNOW?

You may have noticed that the word "adjective" ends with the letters of the suffix *ive*, but it is a noun rather than an adjective. In this instance we have to add the suffix *al* to make the noun "adjective" an adjective: It was an adjectival phrase.

OLD ENGLISH ORIGIN

less

Meaning: **without**

less changes words into adjectives. It is an easy suffix to use because you just add it with no change to the root word. But that is no reason to be careless!

home**less**

home + less
Literal meaning: without (a) home

without a home

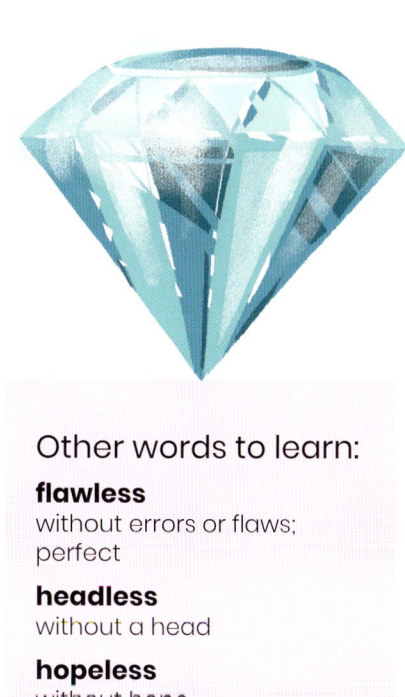

Other words to learn:

flawless
without errors or flaws; perfect

headless
without a head

hopeless
without hope

lifeless
without life

pointless
without a point

thankless
without thanks

help**less**

help (assistance) + less
Literal meaning: without assistance

unable to do anything to assist or help yourself or anyone else

fear**less**

fear + less
Literal meaning: without fear

without fear

thought**less**

thought + less
Literal meaning: without thought

not thinking about others; doing something without thinking about the consequences

DID YOU KNOW?
less is the opposite of the suffix ful as explored on page 140.

ous

Meaning: **full of, having to do with**

ous changes nouns into adjectives. When added to words ending in 'e', the 'e' is dropped: "fame" becomes "famous". When added to a word ending with 'y' pronounced /ee/, the 'y' changes to the letter 'i', and 'ous' is added.

hazardous

hazard (chance) + ous
Literal meaning: having to do with chance of harm

very dangerous

nervous

nerv (e) + ous
Literal meaning: having to do with nerves

very worried or anxious

ambitious

ambiti (go around) + ous
Literal meaning: going around to try and get people to vote for you

having a strong wish to be powerful, rich, or successful

famous

fam (talk, tell) + ous
Literal meaning: much talked about

very well known by many people

Other words to learn:

advantageous (note the exception here: + ous without dropping the e)
favourable to you

cautious
taking note of risk

enormous
extremely large

hilarious
extremely funny

jealous
wanting something that someone else has

mysterious
puzzling or strange

FUN FACT!

The most hazardous activities include scuba diving and BASE jumping (when you jump from a fixed object such as a building, using a parachute to descend safely to the ground). Also on the list are hang-gliding, racing car driving, flying a plane, horse riding, bungee jumping, parasailing and off-roading. Any extreme sport that you do alone, like solo free-climbing, is also considered extremely dangerous. Which would make you most nervous?

OLD ENGLISH ORIGIN

ly

Meaning: **like**

ly changes a noun or adjective into an adverb.
An adverb tells us how something is done.

proud**ly**

proud + ly
Literal meaning: in the manner of being proud

with a sense of happiness and satisfaction

gent**ly**

gent + l(e) + y
Literal meaning: in the manner of softness

in a calm and controlled manner

speedi**ly**

speed(y) + i + ly
Literal meaning: having to with speed

fast

brave**ly**

brave + ly
Literal meaning: in the manner of being brave

with courage

ADVERB SUFFIXES

If a word uses a suffix to turn itself into an adverb, that suffix is called an adverb suffix. They usually change an adjective into an adverb. The most common suffixes are *ly*, *ily*, *ally*, *wise* and *wards*. Compared to prefixes and other types of suffixes, there really aren't that many.

Other words to learn:

confidently
with trust in self or others

happily
with joy

hesitatingly
with nervousness or caution

loudly
with volume

quietly
without noise

wildly
with uncontrolled or powerful energy

wards

Meaning: **direction**

wards changes a word into an adverb. This adverb tells us about the direction something or someone is moving in.

up**wards**

up + wards
Literal meaning: turn up

towards a higher place or position

for**wards**

for + wards
Literal meaning: turn towards the front

towards the way you are facing

back**wards**

back + wards
Literal meaning: turn to the back

away from the way you are facing

down**wards**

down + wards
Literal meaning: turn down

towards a lower place or position

Other words to learn:

eastwards
in the direction of East

northwards
in the direction of North

southwards
in the direction of South

westwards
in the direction of West

windwards
facing the wind

CHALLENGE!

You may have heard the expression, "Two steps forward, one step back." What do you think it means?

making progress, but facing problems along the way

FUN FACT!

If you suspend a strong magnet from a cotton thread, it will work just like a compass because it aligns to the Earth's magnetic field. It can tell you if you are moving in a particular direction: northwards, eastwards, southwards, or westwards. We can also say northerly, easterly, southerly, or westerly.

OLD ENGLISH ORIGIN

ways/wise

Meaning: **with respect to, or in the manner of**

ways/**wise** changes a word into an adverb. This adverb tells us about direction and the manner of a verb in a similar way to the suffix *wards* (page 148).

street**wise**

street + wise
Literal meaning: street smart

being smart about how things work in city, like knowing safe and unsafe places

like**wise**

like (same) + wise
Literal meaning: in the same way

in the same way

side**ways**

side + ways
Literal meaning: to move to the side

to move to the left or the right

clock**wise**

clock + wise
Literal meaning: with clock hand direction

a direction that is the same as the way the hands of a clock move

DID YOU KNOW?

The words "ways" and "wise" exist as words in their own right, but with different meanings. We can find our way using a map and we can look both ways when we cross the road. We may know that owls are considered to be wise, or we may know someone who is wise. These uses and meanings of these words are different from their use as suffixes.

Other words to learn:

agewise
in relation to age

always
every time

colourwise
in relation to colour

crosswise
diagonally

lengthwise
in the direction of the longest side

otherwise
differently

FUN FACT!

The sidewinder rattlesnake and a crab can both move sideways very fast. The snake does this by bending its body into a curve and passing the curves down its body. It lifts some of its body up from the ground to ensure that it moves sideways rather than straight ahead. Crabs have their legs on the sides of their bodies and their knees bend outwards, so they can only move sideways.

Subject learning

CHALLENGE!
Why not create your own list of verbs that help with the focus of your learning? Or add at least two more verbs to each column of the table.

Verbs that will help with learning outcomes

Subject maps for:

English

Maths

Science

Geography

History

Art and Design

Verbs that will help with learning outcomes

Depending on what you are learning or have been asked to do, this table will help you focus on the really important part of the task: the verb! The verb tells you what to do and will help you achieve your learning outcome.

Remember	Practise/ Understand	Apply	Create	Explore	Review
arrange	classify	appraise	construct	debate	assess
compare	compare	classify	design	discuss	commit
define	define	construct	develop	estimate	compare
describe	describe	demonstrate	imagine	find	conclude
identify	establish	discuss	invent	imagine	consider
label	explain	explain	make	predict	contrast
list	identify	identify	modify	pretend	evaluate
locate	illustrate	illustrate	organise	produce	present
name	listen	model	plan	qualify	publish
recite	organise	report	produce	question	rate
repeat	practise	rewrite	question	seek	recommend
select	report	sequence	sketch	solve	reflect
sequence	say	show	structure	support	scrutinise
summarise	summarise	structure	think	wonder	summarise

Focus applies to all as understanding these verbs will help you focus on the learning outcomes.

Subject maps

Subject and curriculum words that will help with learning outcomes

Skill
listening
reading
speaking
writing

Reading
decoding – word reading
comprehension
reading for pleasure
reading for information

Language
vocabulary
encoding – word spelling
spelling
punctuation
grammar

English

Reading genres
genres
text types
narrative texts
stories
information
non-fiction
fiction
poems

Writing
handwriting
drafting
editing
composition
transcription
procedure
description
report
explanation
exposition

Maths

Number
even
odd
ordinals
number bonds
place value
addition
subtraction
division
multiplication

Statistics

Measurement

Decimals

Multiplication table

Algebra

Fractions

Rotations

Percentages

Position and direction

Proportion

Calculation

Ratio

Shapes and space
2D shapes
3D shapes
symmetry
polygons

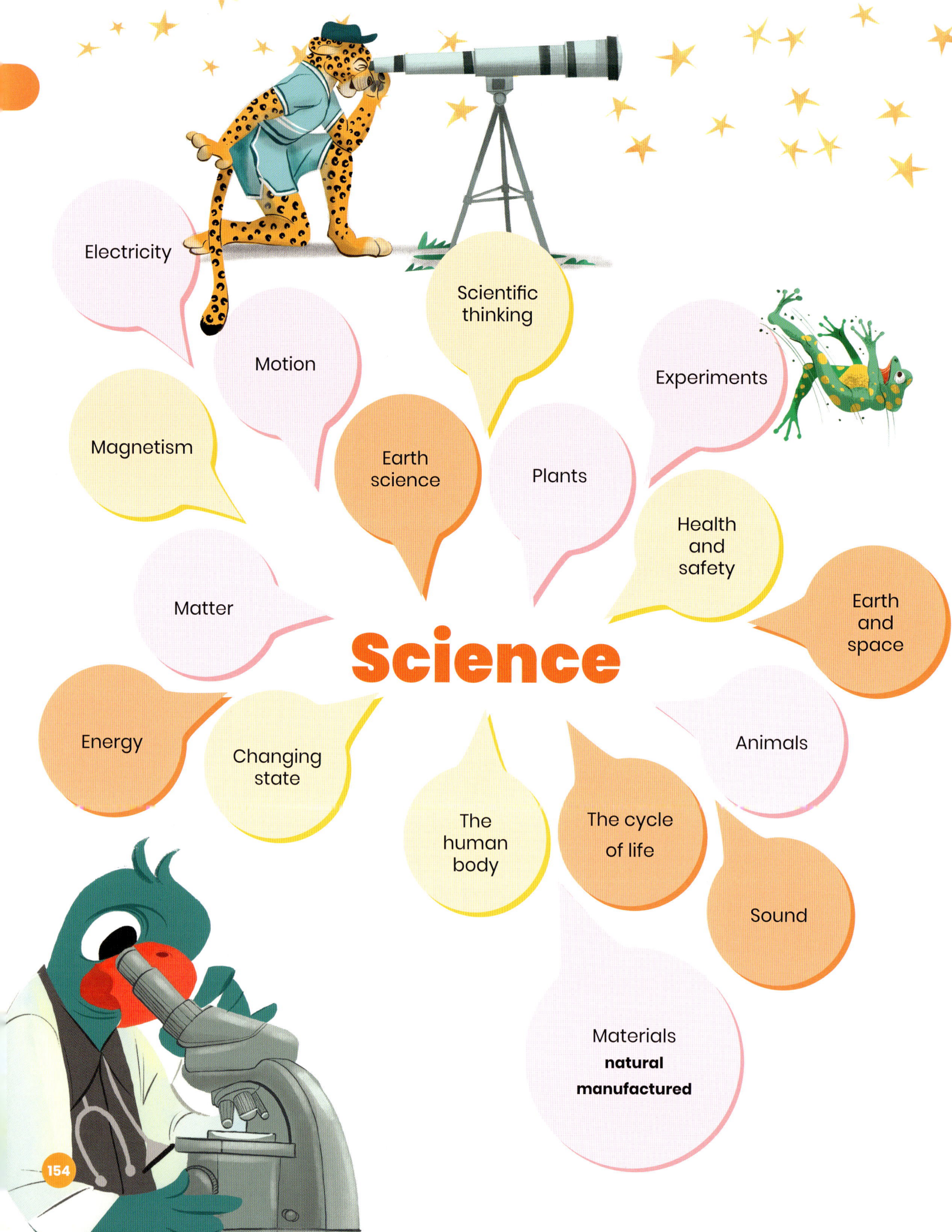

Science

Electricity

Motion

Scientific thinking

Experiments

Magnetism

Earth science

Plants

Health and safety

Matter

Earth and space

Energy

Changing state

The human body

The cycle of life

Animals

Sound

Materials
natural
manufactured

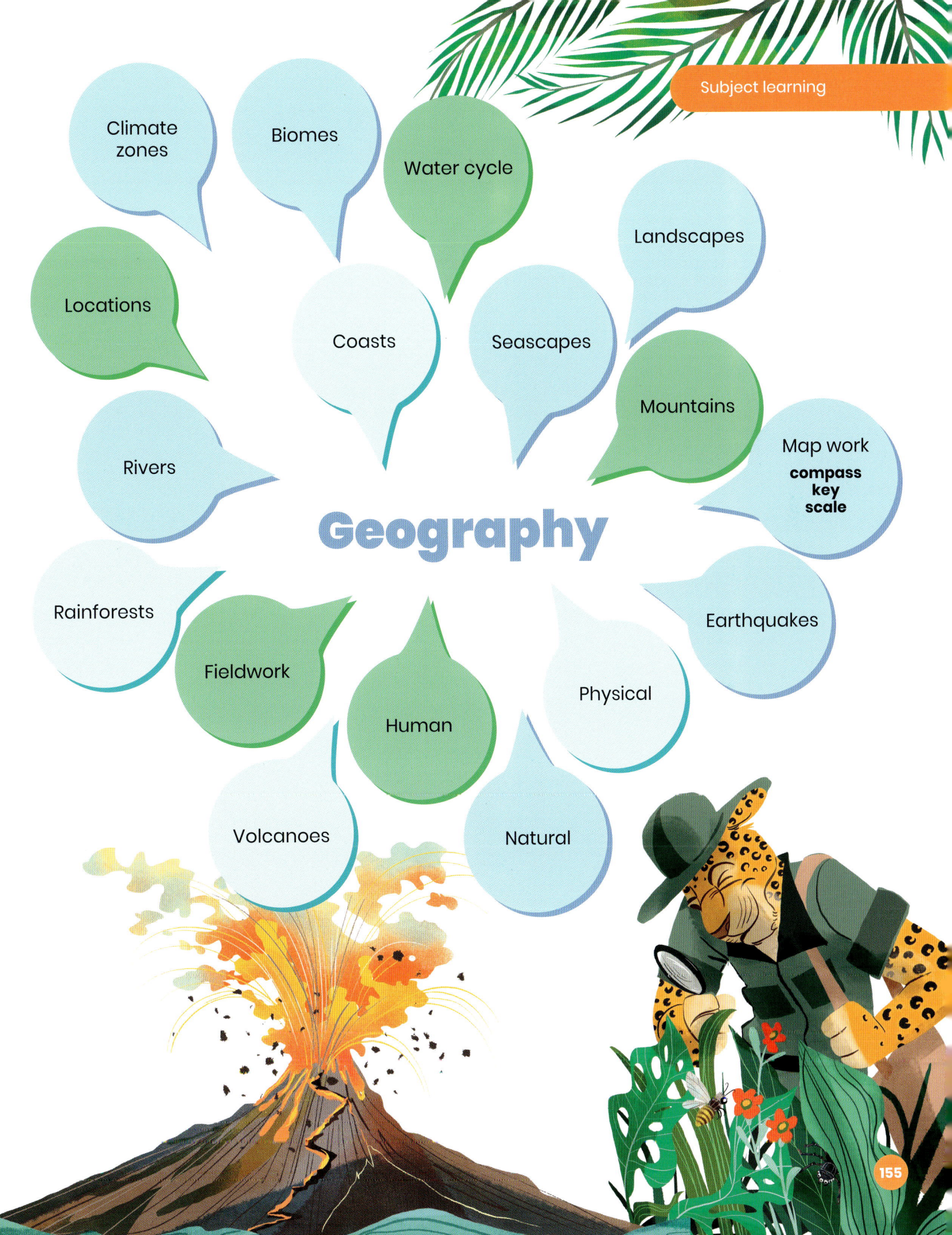

Climate zones

Biomes

Water cycle

Landscapes

Locations

Coasts

Seascapes

Mountains

Map work
**compass
key
scale**

Rivers

Geography

Rainforests

Fieldwork

Human

Physical

Earthquakes

Volcanoes

Natural

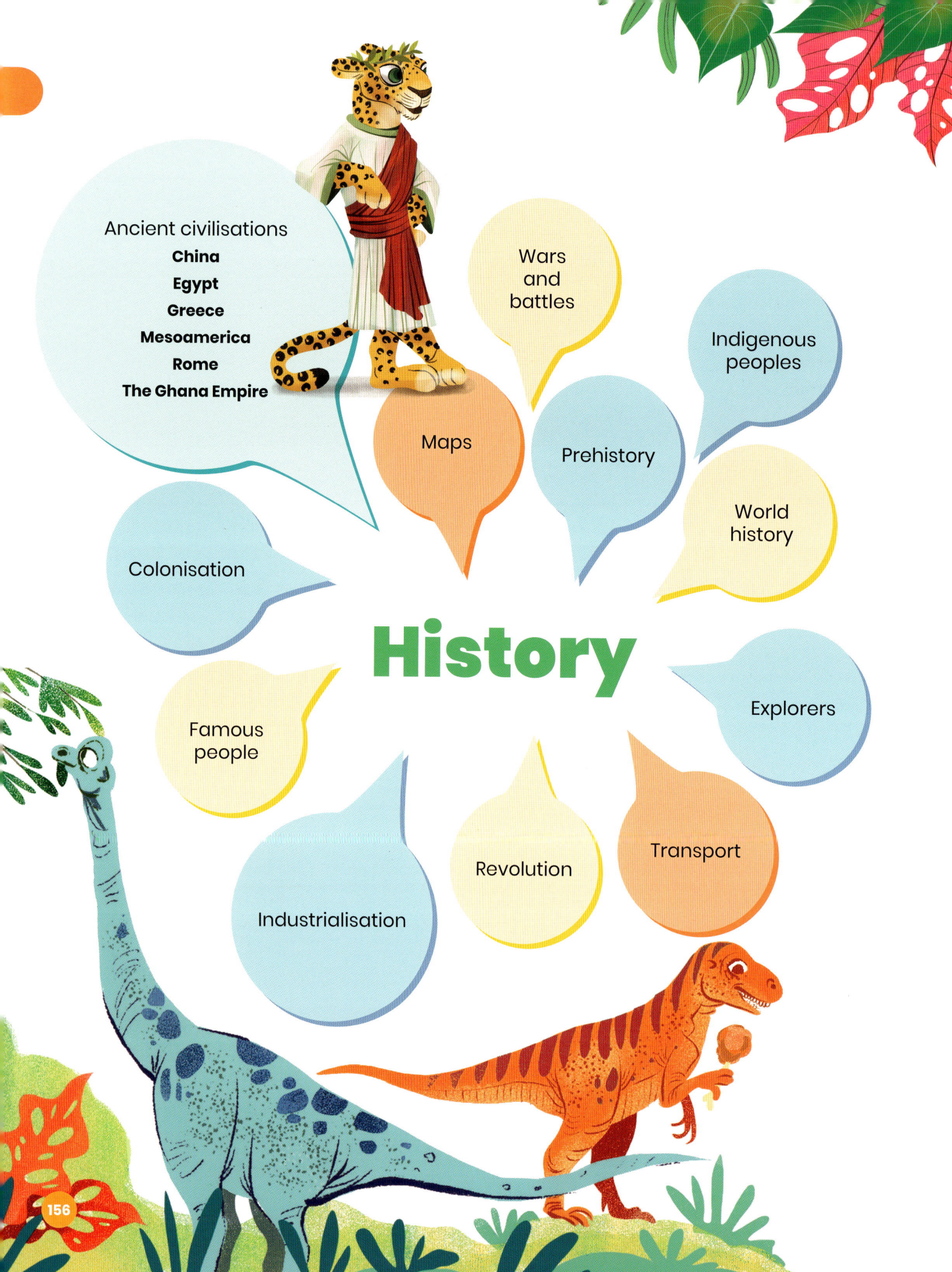

History

Ancient civilisations
- China
- Egypt
- Greece
- Mesoamerica
- Rome
- The Ghana Empire

Wars and battles

Maps

Prehistory

Indigenous peoples

World history

Colonisation

Explorers

Famous people

Industrialisation

Revolution

Transport

Painting
paint
colour, palette
fresco
mural
abstract
impressionism

Drawing
pattern, shape
space, form, texture, tone
perspective
tools: pencil, charcoal
cross-hatching

Sculpture
clay
concrete
wood
metal

Art and Design

Collage
mosaic
montage
tessellation
mixed media

Artists
media
techniques
disciplines
artisan

157

Morpheme maps

How morpheme maps work

Morpheme maps for roots and base words

CHALLENGE!

When you've explored the morpheme maps on the following pages, why not try to build one of your own? You could begin with a root, like *uni* or a base word, like *agree*.

How morpheme maps work

A morpheme is the smallest unit of meaning within a word. Morpheme mapping is when we break down a word into its smallest parts (deconstruction), or build it up into its largest parts (construction). It's a great way to understand how words work!

Morpheme maps provide a visual guide to the ways in which words (roots or base words) can be built using prefixes and suffixes.

- To understand how words are made
- To learn new words (often linked to those you already know)
- To spell and read words more confidently

On the following pages there are:

- Five morpheme maps for each of the roots: *flor*, *rupt*, *spect*, *struct* and *uni*
- Five morpheme maps for each of the base words: *joy*, *thanks*, *sign*, *graph* and *quest*

The root or base word is usually placed centrally and the associated morphemes are shown either side of it.

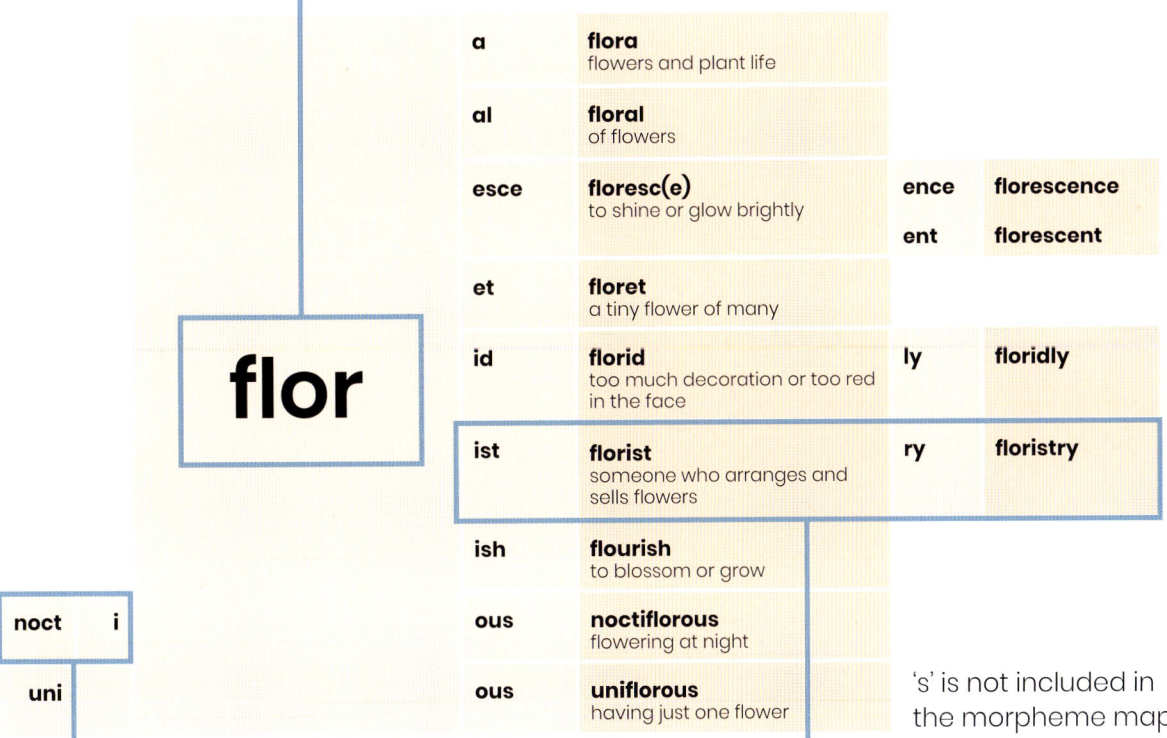

a	**flora** flowers and plant life		
al	**floral** of flowers		
esce	**floresc(e)** to shine or glow brightly	ence	**florescence**
		ent	**florescent**
et	**floret** a tiny flower of many		
id	**florid** too much decoration or too red in the face	ly	**floridly**
ist	**florist** someone who arranges and sells flowers	ry	**floristry**
ish	**flourish** to blossom or grow		
ous	**noctiflorous** flowering at night		
ous	**uniflorous** having just one flower		

flor

noct | i

uni

's' is not included in the morpheme maps.

Prefixes to the left and **suffixes** to the right! The general rule is to still read from left to right to gradually build the word by adding the morphemes shown.

flor

Meaning: **flower**

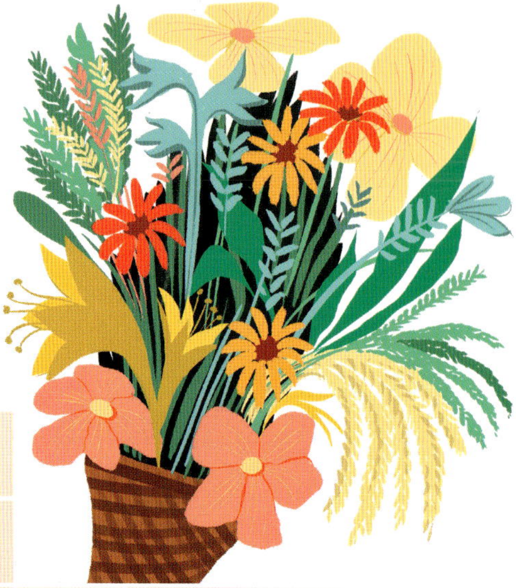

a	**flora** flowers and plant life			
al	**floral** of flowers			
esce	**floresc(e)** to shine or glow brightly	ence	**florescence**	
		ent	**florescent**	
et	**floret** a tiny flower of many			
id	**florid** too much decoration or too red in the face	ly	**floridly**	
ist	**florist** someone who arranges and sells flowers	ry	**floristry**	
ish	**flourish** to blossom or grow			
ous	**noctiflorous** flowering at night			
ous	**uniflorous** having just one flower			

noct · i

uni

flor

DID YOU KNOW?

Did you know? La Florida is the original Spanish name for the state of Florida in the US. It means "place of flowers".

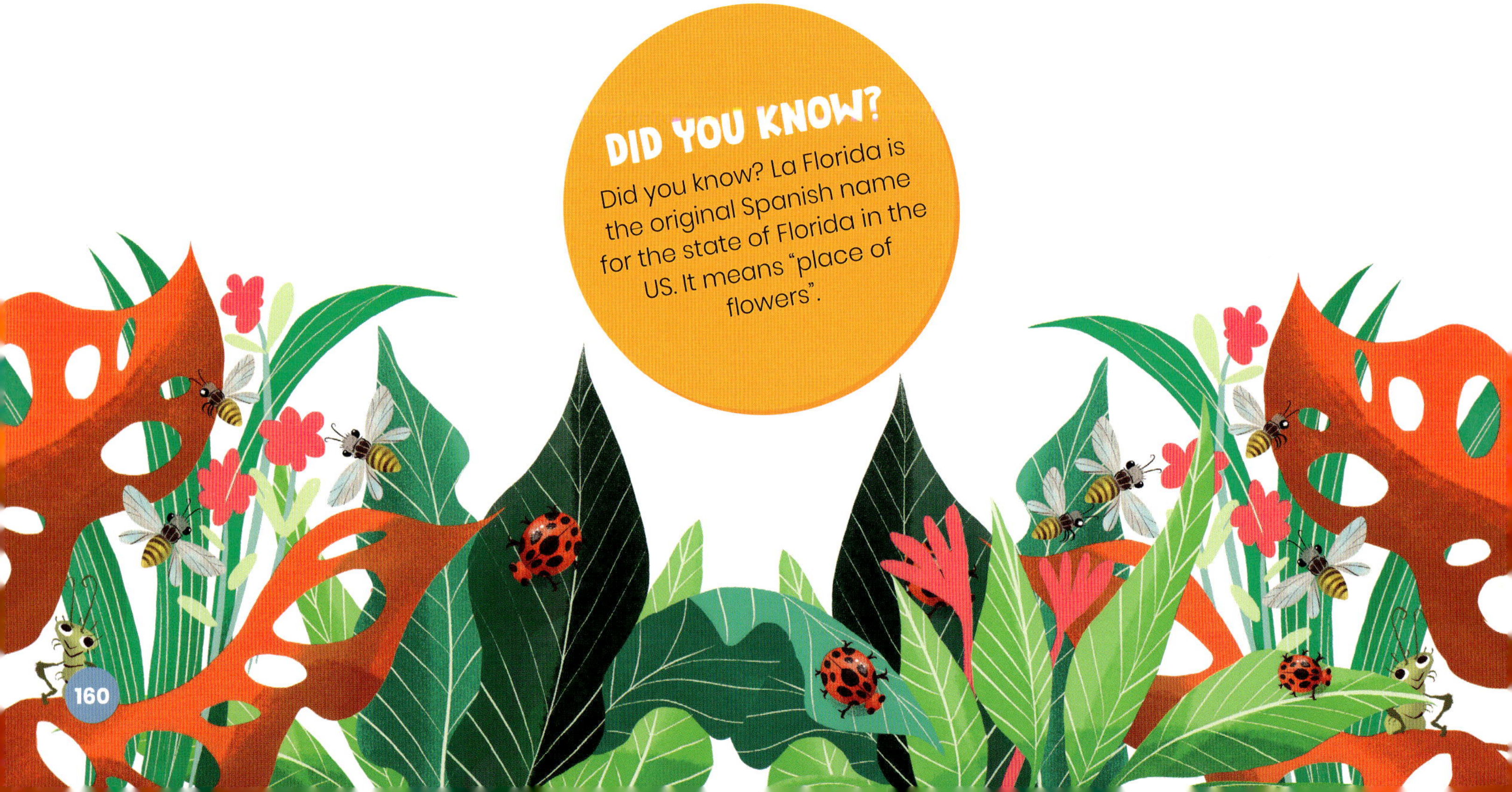

rupt

Meaning: **break**

bank		**bankrupt** having no money to pay what you owe	cy	**bankruptcy**
			ed	**bankrupted**
ab		**abrupt** sudden and unpleasantly unexpected	ly	**abruptly**
			ness	**abruptness**
cor		**corrupt** dishonest, bad	ed	**corrupted**
			ible	**corruptible**
			ing	**corrupting**
			ion	**corruption**
			ly	**corruptly**
dis		**disrupt** to prevent something from continuing in the usual way	ed	**disrupted**
			ing	**disrupting**
	rupt		ion	**disruption**
			ive	**disruptive**
			or	**disruptor**
e		**erupt** to start suddenly and violently	ed	**erupted**
			ing	**erupting**
			ion	**eruption**
inter		**interrupt** to stop something from happening for a short time	ed	**interrupted**
			ible	**interruptible**
			ing	**interrupting**
			ion	**interruption**
		ure	**rupture** to cause something to explode or break	ed	**ruptured**
				ing	**rupturing**

spect

Meaning: **a public show or to do with sight**

dis	re		**respect** to speak or behave politely to someone	ed	**respected**		
				ing	**respecting**		
				ful	**respectful**		
				fully	**respectfully**		
			disrespect to speak or behave rudely to someone	ed	**disrespected**		
				ing	**disrespecting**		
				ful	**disrespectful**		
				fully	**disrespectfully**		
	in	**spect**	**inspect** to look at something or someone carefully with purpose	ed	**inspected**		
				or	**inspector**		
				ing	**inspecting**		
				ion	**inspection**		
	intro		**introspect** to consider your ideas, thoughts and feelings	ed	**introspected**		
				ion	**introspection**		
				ive	**introspective**		
	per		**(perspect)**	ive	**perspective** a particular way of considering something		
				acle	**spectacle** an unusual event that attracts attention	ular	**spectacular**	ly	**spectacularly**
				ate	**spectate** to watch	or	**spectator**	ship	**spectatorship**
				re	**spectre** something that causes fear		

LATIN ORIGIN

struct

Meaning: **to form or build**

prefix	prefix	word	suffix	result	suffix	result
		construct to build, form	ed	constructed		
			ing	constructing		
			ion	construction		
			ive	constructive		
re	con	**reconstruct**	ed	reconstructed		
			ing	reconstructing		
			ion	reconstruction		
			ive	reconstructive		
de		**deconstruct**	ed	deconstructed		
			ing	deconstructing		
			ion	deconstruction		
			ive	deconstructive		
	de	**destruct** to destroy	ion	destruction		
			ive	destructive		
			ible	destructible		
	ob	**obstruct** to block	ed	obstructed		
			ing	obstructing		
			ion	obstruction		
			ive	obstructive		
	in	**instruct** to tell someone what to do	ed	instructed		
			ing	instructing		
			ion	instruction		
			ive	instructive		
			or	instructor		
super			ure	**superstructure** the part of a building above its foundation		
infra			ure	**infrastructure** the basic structure of a building or system		
			ure	**structure** to arrange the parts of something or the way parts are arranged	ed	structured
					ing	structuring
					al	structural

163

uni

Meaning: **one**

t	**unit** a measure		
te	**unite** to come together as one	**ed**	**united**
		fy	**unify**
		ing	**uniting**
on	**union** joining together		
lateral	**unilateral** by one only	**ly**	**unilaterally**
que	**unique** distinctively different	**ness**	**uniqueness**
verse	**universe** everything that exists	**al**	**universal**
		ally	**universally**
		sity	**university**
corn	**unicorn** mythical one- horned creature		
cycle	**unicycle** one-wheeled transport	**ing**	**unicycling**
form	**uniform** one and the same	**ed**	**uniformed**

uni

FUN FACT!

The oldest existing university in the world is the University of Karueein in Fez, Morocco. It has been functioning as a university nonstop since 859 CE.

joy

Meaning: **pleasure and delight**

en		**enjoy** to take delight in	ed	enjoyed	
			ing	enjoying	
			ment	enjoyment	
			able	enjoyable	
			ably	enjoyably	
over		**overjoy** to give great joy or take delight in	ed	overjoyed	
			ment	over-enjoyment	
re	**joy**	**rejoice** to celebrate			
		joyful full of joy	ly	joyfully	
ful			ness	joyfulness	
ous		**joyous** happy, cheerful	ly	joyously	
			ness	joyousness	
less		**joyless** to lack joy	ly	joylessly	
			ness	joylessness	

thank

Meaning: **to appreciate or show gratitude**

thank	ful	thankful full of joy	ly	thankfully	
			ness	thankfulness	
	ed	thanked			
	ing	thanking			
	less	thankless	ness	thanklessness	
un		(unthank)	ful	unthankful	ly	unthankfully

FUN FACT!

The National Turkey Foundation states that as many as 88% of Americans eat turkey for the Thanksgiving celebratory meal. This has remained constant despite trends to eat alternatives to meat.

DID YOU KNOW?

If someone says, "Thank your lucky stars", they mean that you should be very grateful for something, because it could have easily turned out differently.

LATIN ORIGIN

sign

Meaning: **an indication or to mark**

counter		**countersign** to sign when another has already signed		
con		**consign** to send something to someone	ment	**consignment**
de	**sign**	**design** to plan something and draw up a plan for it	er	**designer**
			ate	**designate**
			ed	**designed**
			ing	**designing**
re		**resign** to leave a job or give up on something	ed	**resigned**
			ing	**resigning**
		ed	**signed**	
		ing	**signing**	
		al	**signal** a gesture, sound or action for another	ed	**signalled**
				ing	**signalling**
		ify	**signify** a sign to communicate a particular meaning	ing	**signifying**
			(i)cant	**significant**	ly	**significantly**
		ature	**signature** to write your own name		

FUN FACT!

Ship flag signs are known as maritime signal flags. There are 40 flags that, when combined, can create messages that use universal language and can be understood by any ship around the world. Signal flags are still used despite the rise of electronic communication.

CHALLENGE!

If you add the prefix *in* to "significantly", what word do you make? What change in meaning does the prefix *in* make?

———

insignificantly. The change makes the word mean 'not'.

graph

Meaning: **to write, draw, or measure**

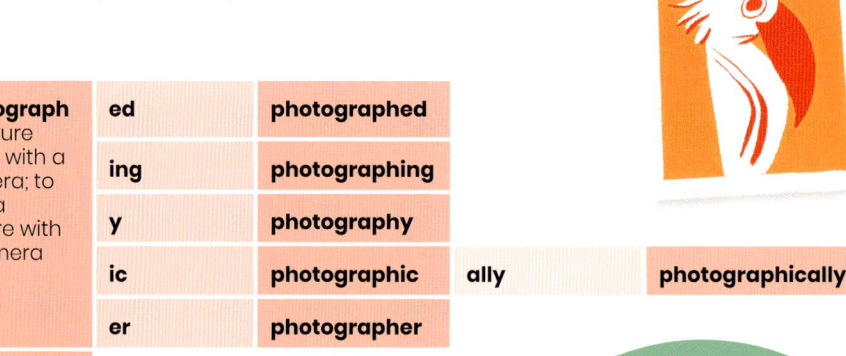

photo	graph	**photograph** a picture taken with a camera; to take a picture with a camera	ed	**photographed**		
			ing	**photographing**		
			y	**photography**		
			ic	**photographic**	ally	**photographically**
			er	**photographer**		
para		**paragraph** a section of writing within a longer piece of writing				
auto		**autograph** a writing of your own name in your own style	ed	**autographed**		
			ing	**autographing**		
bio		**biography** the story of someone's life	y			
		biographer	er			
		biographic	ic		al	**biographical**
					ally	**biographically**
geo		**geography** the study of earth and everything on it	y			
		geographer	er			
		geographic	ic		ally	**geographically**
		graphic clear in pictures	ic			
		graphical	al			

CHALLENGE!

If you add the prefix *auto* to "biography", what word do you make? What change in meaning does the prefix *auto* make?

autobiography. The change makes the word mean "of self".

LATIN ORIGIN

quest

Meaning: **to seek or search**

con	**conquest** a win			
re	**request** to ask	ed	requested	
		ing	requesting	
in	**inquest** an official examination of facts to discover the cause of something			
un	**quest**	ion	(unquestion)	ed	unquestioned

ion	(unquestion)	ed	unquestioned
		ing	unquestioning
		able	unquestionable without any doubt
	question to ask	er	questioner
		ed	questioned
		ing	questioning
		able	questionable
		aire	questionnaire

DID YOU KNOW?
The question mark began as a word, *quaestio*, and was written at the end of a sentence. Over time, it was shortened to *qu*, and later, into the punctuation mark we recognise and use today: **?**

FUN FACT!
Moby Dick, The Lord of the Rings, Alice's Adventures in Wonderland, and the Harry Potter books, are all classified as quests. Many online games and e-sports offer virtual quests. Space exploration is still a quest for humans.

169

Word lists

Irregular verb list

Weekly spelling lists

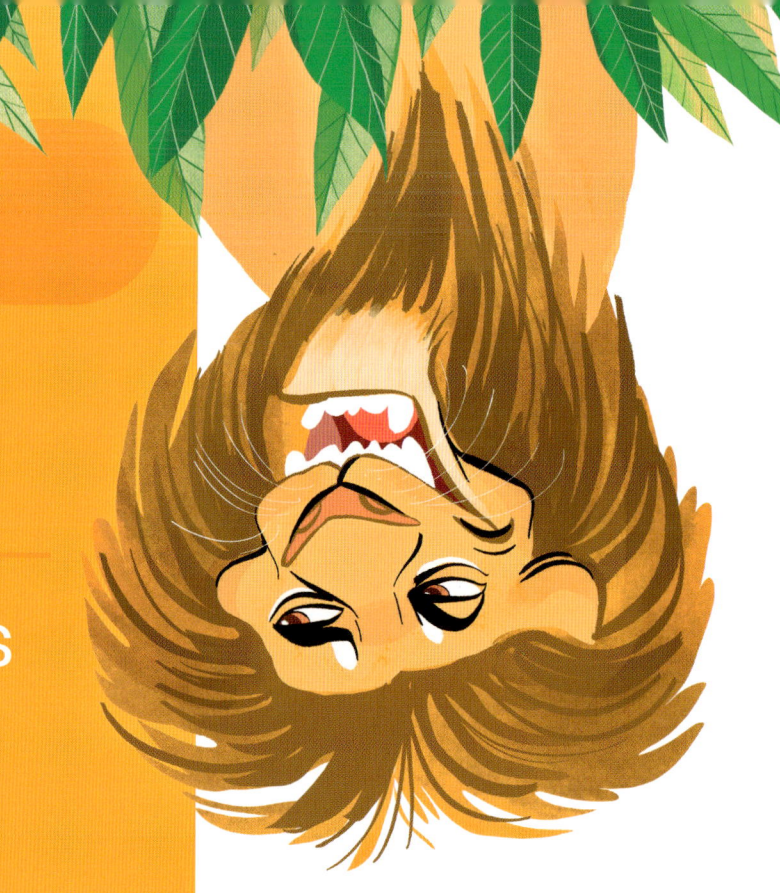

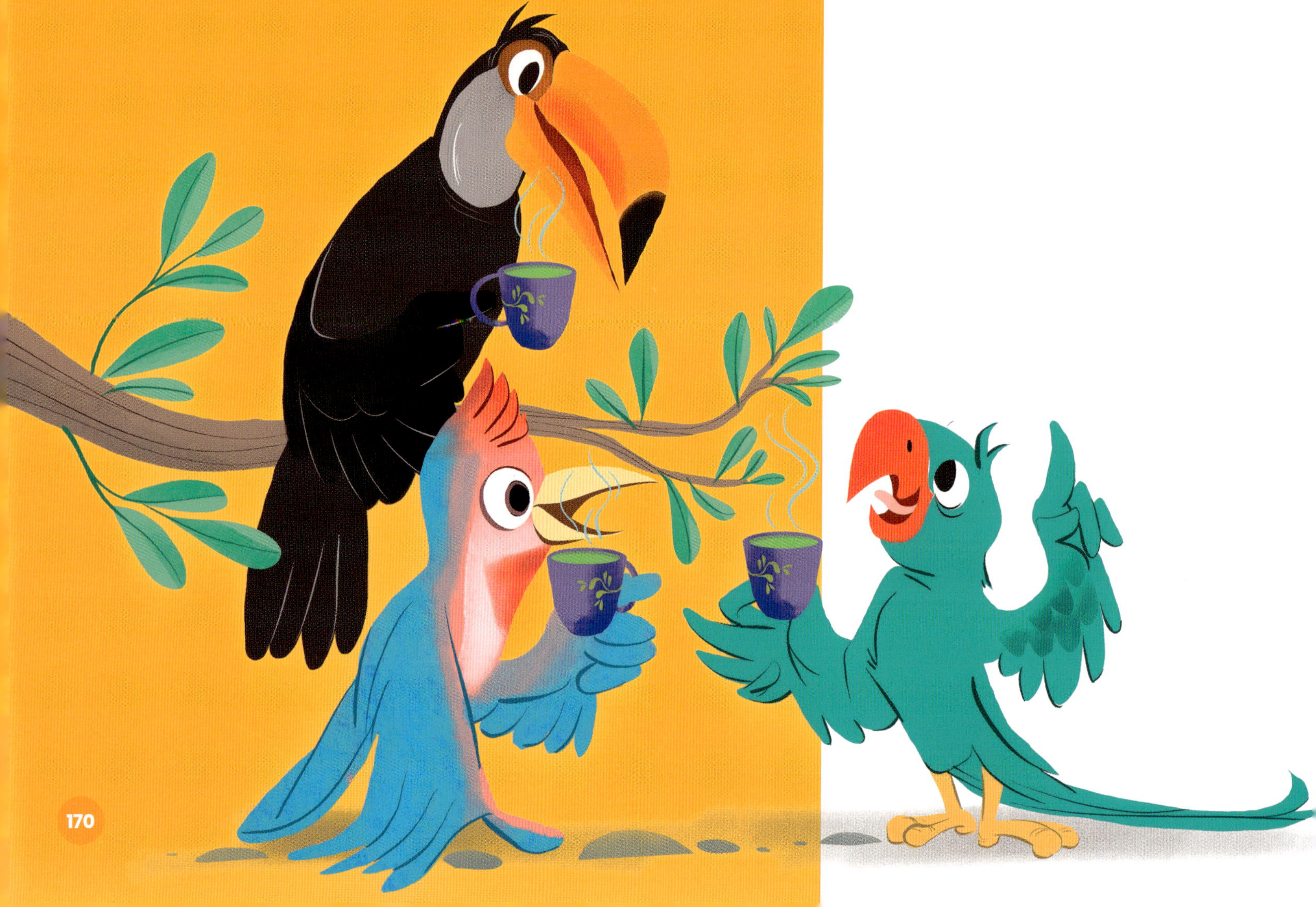

Irregular verb list

The verb **have** is used on its own and with other verbs. It doesn't change for the different pronouns. The pronouns are **I**, **you**, **he**, **she**, **it**, **we, you** (plural) and **they**.

I had	we had
you had	you had
he, she, it had	they had

The verb **be** is used on its own and with other verbs. It changes for some pronouns:

I was	we were
you were	you were
he, she, it was	they were

Some verbs only change in pronunciation.
Did you **read** (Say: **reed**) that carefully?
Yes, we **read** (Say: **red**) it very carefully!

Some verbs are the same in the present and past tense. Many end in **t**.

Present tense	Past simple	Past participle
set	set	set
hit	hit	hit
cut	cut	cut
shut	shut	shut

The past participle is a verb form that is used when you're using the past tense but talking about something that happened at an even earlier time. It's always combined with a form of "have". For example: "Yesterday, I ate more bananas than I had eaten the day before."

Here are some more **examples of irregular verbs**. For irregular verbs in the past tense, we just have to find a way to learn them. The more you use them, the more you'll remember them!

Present tense	Past simple	Past participle
become	became	become
break	broke	broken
bring	brought	brought
buy	bought	bought
can	could	been able to
catch	caught	caught
choose	chose	chosen
do	did	done
draw	drew	drawn
drink	drank	drunk
eat	ate	eaten
get	got	got
go	went	been
grow	grew	grown
hear	heard	heard
know	knew	known
run	ran	run
say	said	said
see	saw	seen
throw	threw	thrown
understand	understood	understood
write	wrote	written

Weekly spelling lists

It's useful to know more about where words come from to help you to have a richer vocabulary, and to help with reading, writing, and spelling, too. Sometimes it's helpful to just learn a group of words so they stick in your memory – practice makes perfect! Here are 30 lists of words that you may find handy to learn. They are linked to a root or base word, and many use prefixes and suffixes.

List 1: aqua (relating to water)

aquamarine	aqua
aquatic	aqueous
aquarium	aqueduct
Aquarius	Aquarian
aqualung	aquaplane

List 2: bene (kindness, doing well)

benefit	benefitting
benevolent	benevolence
benefactor	benevolently
beneficial	benefitting
beneficiary	beneficiaries

List 3: cap (the top, end)

capital	capitalise
captain	capture
chapter	caption
capacity	encapsulate
capitulate	capitulation

List 4: dia (across)

diameter	diametrical
diagonal	diagonally
diagram	diagrammatic
dialogue	dialogical
diagnose	diagnostic

List 5: equi (equal)

equal	equality
equivalent	equivocal
equilateral	equidistant
equilibrium	equator
adequate	equate

List 6: flex (to bend)

flexible	inflexible
flexibility	reflection
reflect	reflective
deflect	deflection
genuflect	reflexive

List 7: gen (beget, to generate something)

genes	genetic
genre	engender
general	generalisation
genuine	gentle
generate	generation

List 8: imag (likeness)

image	imagery
imagine	imagination
imaginary	imaginative
self-image	imaging
imagined	imagist

List 9: kryptos (hidden, secret)

crypt	cryptic
cryptography	cryptogram
cryptographic	crypto
encrypt	encryption
decrypt	decryption

List 10: hipp (horse)

hippopotamus	hippopotami
hippodrome	hippiatric
hippology	hippologist
hippomania	hippomaniac
Phillip	Philippa

List 11: junct (join)

junction	juncture
conjunct	conjunction
disjuncture	disjunction
adjunct	injunction
subjunctive	conjunctivitis

List 12: lab (work, toil)

labour	labourer
laboured	labouring
laboratory	laborious
collaborate	collaboration
elaborate	elaboration

List 13: magna (great or large)

magnificent	magnificence
magnify	magnificently
magnification	magnitude
magnate	magnum
magnanimity	magnanimous

List 14: nom (name)

nominal	nominate
nominee	denominate
denominator	denomination
misnomer	prenominated
nomenclature	nom de plume

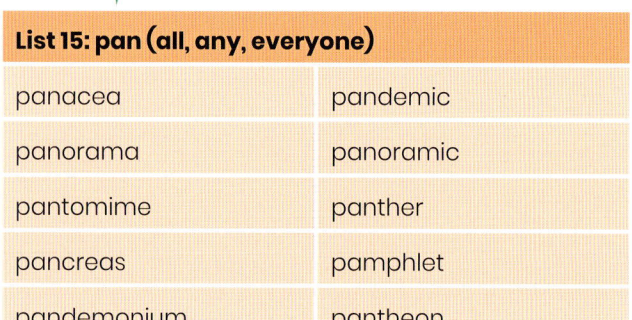

List 15: pan (all, any, everyone)

panacea	pandemic
panorama	panoramic
pantomime	panther
pancreas	pamphlet
pandemonium	pantheon

List 16: mal (bad)

malfunction	malady
malcontent	malaise
malicious	maligned
malevolent	malpractice
malformed	malnutrition

List 17: -oid (like, resembling)

asteroid	cuboid
humanoid	ovoid
planetoid	android
factoid	fibroid
tabloid	paranoid

List 18: pel (to drive, force)

repel	repellent
expel	impel
compel	compelling
propel	propeller
dispel	catapult

List 19: quad (four)

quads	quadruple
quadrant	quad bike
quadrilateral	quadratic
quadriceps	squad
quadrangle	quadrangular

List 20: san (health)

sanitation	sanitary
sanity	sanitise
insanity	sanitorium
sanctify	sane
insane	unsanitary

List 21: scene (stage setting)

scene	scenery
scenic	scenario
sceneries	scenically
scent	scented
scenographer	scenography

List 22: reg (rule, guide, direct)

regular	regulate
regulation	regulatory
deregulate	regiment
regionalism	region
irregular	arrogant

List 23: scend (to climb, go)

ascend	ascension
descend	descendant
condescend	condescending
transcend	transcendent
crescendo	crescendos

List 24: tact, tang (to touch)

tactile	tangible
intact	intangible
tactless	tangent
tactful	tangentially
contact	intangibility

List 25: uni (one)

unify	union
unique	unison
uniform	unicycle
universe	unit
unite	universal

List 26: viv (to live)

revive	revival
survive	survivor
vital	vitality
convivial	conviviality
vivid	revitalise

List 27: -y (nouns)

melody	malady
ability	academy
beauty	duty
energy	assembly
theory	symmetry

List 28: vince/vic (to conquer)

convince	convincing
invincible	invincibility
province	provincial
victory	victorious
victor	evict

List 29: -y (adjectives)

hungry	lovely
luxury	misery
ready	dowdy
flaky	gaudy
queasy	sturdy

List 30: zoo (animal, life)

zoo	zoos
zoologist	zookeeper
zoological	zoology
azoic	zodiac
protozoa	Zoe

About the **author**

Gill Budgell is an experienced educator and author. She specialises in early years and primary English literacy and language development for first language and bilingual learners. Gill has developed, written, and published many outstanding and award-winning print and digital resources.

This book focuses on supporting children aged 7–11 to better understand the origins and building blocks of words. We know from research that talking from as early as possible in life increases active vocabulary, and an increased vocabulary unlocks richer language development and communication. The benefits of knowing and understanding more words, as well as how they are created and linked to other similar words across speaking, reading, writing and spelling, is indisputable. A broad vocabulary can assist children in accessing their education more easily, helping them to sort learning into categories, as well as to see overlaps between different subjects.

While reflecting on **Where Words Come From**, Gill says: "This book is a landmark publication in providing an accessible route into a rich and complex subject. It will help children to unlock the code of words we use: their roots, meanings and associations. This book is a great place to begin to spark children's curiosity about words and for them to begin their etymological adventure."